LIBRARY MANUALS

Volume 5

FUNDAMENTALS OF PRACTICAL CATALOGUING

FUNDAMENTALS OF PRACTICAL CATALOGUING

MARGARET S. TAYLOR

LONDON AND NEW YORK

First published in 1948 by George Allen & Unwin Ltd

This edition first published in 2022
by Routledge
4 Park Square, Milton Park, Abingdon, Oxon OX14 4RN

and by Routledge
605 Third Avenue, New York, NY 10017

Routledge is an imprint of the Taylor & Francis Group, an informa business

Copyright © 1948 by Taylor & Francis.

All rights reserved. No part of this book may be reprinted or reproduced or utilised in any form or by any electronic, mechanical, or other means, now known or hereafter invented, including photocopying and recording, or in any information storage or retrieval system, without permission in writing from the publishers.

Trademark notice: Product or corporate names may be trademarks or registered trademarks, and are used only for identification and explanation without intent to infringe.

British Library Cataloguing in Publication Data
A catalogue record for this book is available from the British Library

ISBN: 978-1-03-213109-2 (Set)
ISBN: 978-1-00-322771-7 (Set) (ebk)
ISBN: 978-1-03-213354-6 (Volume 5) (hbk)
ISBN: 978-1-03-213359-1 (Volume 5) (pbk)
ISBN: 978-1-00-322884-4 (Volume 5) (ebk)

DOI: 10.4324/9781003228844

Publisher's Note
The publisher has gone to great lengths to ensure the quality of this reprint but points out that some imperfections in the original copies may be apparent.

Disclaimer
The publisher has made every effort to trace copyright holders and would welcome correspondence from those they have been unable to trace.

FUNDAMENTALS OF PRACTICAL CATALOGUING

by

MARGARET S. TAYLOR
M.A., F.L.A., *Chief Librarian, Merthyr Tydfil*
formerly Lecturer in Cataloguing
and Classification
School of Librarianship
London University, 1935-47

LONDON
GEORGE ALLEN & UNWIN LTD
MUSEUM STREET

First Published in 1948
Second Impression 1954
Third Impression 1963

This book is copyright under the Berne Convention. Apart from any fair dealing for the purposes of private study, research, criticism or review, as permitted under the Copyright Act, 1956, no portion may be reproduced by any process without written permission. Enquiries should be addressed to the Publishers.

Printed in Great Britain by
JOHN DICKENS AND CO LTD, NORTHAMPTON

GENERAL INTRODUCTION

IN the general introduction to the earlier volumes in this series, the original editor, Mr. W. E. Doubleday, wrote:

"This new series of Handbooks is intended to supplement the larger Manuals issued by Messrs. Allen & Unwin and the Library Association.... (It) is issued independently by Messrs. Allen & Unwin, and the range is sufficiently wide to make the volumes appeal to administrators, librarians, assistants, and students who intend to sit at the professional examinations."

Though the main features in the practice of librarianship are not subject to any great change, many of the details of library administration are under a constant process of development which seeks improvement, e.g. of methods of cataloguing, of book classification, of shelf arrangement, and of service to readers. Those may best be dealt with in small monographs which may be revised at sufficiently frequent intervals.

There is a special need for up-to-date material for the use of candidates preparing for Library Association examinations, either by private study, correspondence course, or, more fortunately for them, at one of the full-time schools of librarianship, and it is hoped that this series will prove particularly helpful to them. It is hoped also that the volumes will be found useful to practising librarians, particularly to those engaged in special departments, or in reorganization, or revision of library systems which have become out of date.

November 19, 1947.

INTRODUCTION

A BIBLIOGRAPHY is a list of books or manuscripts on a particular subject, or subjects. A catalogue is also a list but its scope is limited to a particular collection, *e.g. Librorum impressorum qui in Museo Britannico adservantur catalogus*, the *Gesamtkatalog der preussischen Bibliotheken*, the *Index-catalogue of the Library of the Surgeon-General's Office*.

Catalogues were first compiled to serve as records of stock. Even in the days of ancient Egypt and Assyria it was necessary to keep a check on a library's treasures, and this could only be done if the librarian had a complete list of them. Later, the actual location of items was included, especially if some of these were stored in another part of the building. In a monastic library, for example, some books might also be kept in the cloisters and some in the chapel. A more modern development is the bibliographical description of books as well as mere listing. This enables readers to select material from the catalogue itself. By comparing such points as publishers, presence of certain types of illustrations, even pagination and size, a student can tell which of two books on a certain subject is more likely to be useful to him.

A reader may ask for a book by its author's name, by some word in the title, or by its subject, so various types of catalogues have been evolved to satisfy these enquiries. The three basic varieties are (1) the *Author*, which lists books under headings composed of authors' names; (2) the *Title*, where headings consist of words from the titles of books; (3) the *Subject*, where the heading may either be the name of a book's specific subject (*Alphabetical-Subject* catalogue), or the name of a class containing that specific subject (the *Alphabetical-Classed* catalogue), or some symbol taken from a classification scheme which represents the subject (the *Classified catalogue*). Nos. (1) and (2) are usually amalgamated to form a complex type known as the *Author-Title* catalogue. When this and the *Alphabetical-Subject* are mixed, the catalogue is called *Dictionary*.

Physical forms are equally varied. A catalogue may be written, typed, or printed. It may be in the form of a book; in a special kind of loose-leaf binder, known as a sheaf; or it may be on cards which are filed upright in cabinet drawers.

The cataloguer seldom reads a book as part of his official duties. What he does in his spare time is another matter. But to catalogue a book, it is only very occasionally that the text has to be studied. The cataloguer gets his data from the preliminary pages and the appearance of the volume or volumes. Preliminary pages consist of half-title page, frontispiece, title-page, preface or foreword, table of contents, list of illustrations, and introduction by the author. Some of these items may be missing, but, unless the copy is imperfect, a modern book will always have a title-page. This has been an indispensable feature since the sixteenth century. It contains the title in full (including name of author), place of publication, name of publisher, and usually date of publication. There may also be details about the edition and the name of a series to which the book belongs. Before 1520, by which date the presence of a title-page was a regular occurrence, a book usually ended with a statement giving title, author, printer, and date. This was the colophon. It is seldom found in modern works.

After examining the title-page, the cataloguer turns to the half-title page, which precedes it. This gives a short version of the title and may also have the name of the series. After that, he examines the table of contents, etc., and then proceeds to study certain physical features of the volume, such as height, number of pages, etc.

CONTENTS

CHAPTER		PAGE
	GENERAL INTRODUCTION	5
	INTRODUCTION	7
I.	SIMPLE MAIN AUTHOR ENTRIES	11
II.	AUTHOR AND TITLE ADDED ENTRIES	31
III.	AUTHOR REFERENCES	44
IV.	MAIN TITLE ENTRIES	60
V.	CORPORATE AUTHORSHIP	76
VI.	CONTENTS. NOTES. ANALYTICS	91
VII.	SUBJECT CATALOGUING	102
VIII.	ARRANGEMENT AND FILING	120
IX.	SIMPLIFIED CATALOGUING	129
	TERMS AND DEFINITIONS	140
	INDEX	142

CHAPTER I

SIMPLE MAIN AUTHOR ENTRIES

1. THE IMPORTANCE OF RULES AND UNIFORM STYLE

A CATALOGUE is sometimes made and finished by one person, but usually a library keeps on adding new books to its stock and the work of cataloguing continues indefinitely from generation to generation. It is important that new cataloguers should continue the methods of their predecessors, or the catalogue becomes confused and full of inconsistencies. Hence the necessity for rules of entry, arrangement, and style.

While uniformity is essential in the catalogue, or catalogues, of a single library, it is also desirable that other libraries should conform to the same code of rules. Exceptions may be made in the case of special libraries. These vary so widely, both in nature of stock and purposes for which material is required, that individuality of treatment may be necessary. But general libraries in this country would certainly benefit by adopting similar cataloguing methods. A reader gets used to one set of rules for entry and style. When he goes to another library, the catalogue may be quite different and he has to start afresh learning to find his way about that one.

The Library Association and American Library Association Joint Code is the one most commonly used in this country, but it is often applied in a modified form. Many libraries use British Museum, Cutter, or their own rules. Apart from rules for entry, the description of books and cataloguing style generally show lamentable variety in practice. The cataloguer may have to follow the individual method of a particular library when he starts to work there, but when he is a student of cataloguing he must master the most widely used code and practice making entries in a fixed style in conformity with that code. The L.A. and A.L.A. rules (commonly called the A.A. or the Joint Code) have been followed in this book. The American Library Association's "preliminary American second edition" of 1941 is referred to when there are important changes or expansions. A uniform style, in accordance with the Joint Code and the Library of Congress unit cards, has been adopted in all the practical examples.

Full cataloguing is prescribed except in Chapter IX. The student should learn to catalogue in a form that gives detailed descriptions of books. He may later work in a library where this is the practice. On the other hand, if he goes to one where the catalogue is little more than a finding list and book description cut to a minimum, he can soon adapt himself to the shortened form.

2. RULING FOR A CATALOGUE CARD

The standard catalogue card measures 12·5 centimetres across and 7·5 centimetres in height. It stands in a card-cabinet drawer, and about half a centimetre from the bottom of the card there is a punched hole to take a locking rod. This rod prevents unauthorized persons from removing a card. The hole extends upwards for nearly one centimetre, so the cataloguer has a space above of six by twelve and a half centimetres for writing an entry. It is advisable to keep the entry as high up the card as possible, since the bottom half is not easily read when the card is locked into a drawer.

The catalogue presents a much neater and more attractive appearance, besides being easier to consult, if all entry headings and other items begin in the same position. To aid this, the student is advised to rule a line across each card at a distance of one centimetre from the top edge. He should then draw two vertical margins on the left-hand side, the first being one centimetre from the edge and the second two centimetres. The horizontal line is for the main entry heading. The second margin is for beginning each "paragraph" in the description, which otherwise will come up to the first margin. When ruled, a card will look like Example 1 (*see* page 26).

3. THE HEADING

Except for anonymous books, the main entry in an Author-title, or a Dictionary catalogue is made under the person, or persons, or corporate body responsible for the book's existence, *i.e.* its author. Only straightforward examples of individual authorship will be considered for the present.

The author's name is used as heading and is written along the ruled line across the card, starting within the first margin. It normally consists of one or more christian names and a surname, *e.g.* Henry Ralph Plomer. Sometimes the christian names are only represented by initials on the title-page. In that case, the cataloguer should try to find the full name. The beginner may think this is mere pedantry, but he has only to consult the catalogue of a small library for entries under common surnames like Atkinson, Brown, Clarke, etc., to realize the impossibility of separating works by one J. Brown from another unless full christian names are given. Another bad result of initials is that later the author may publish a book which gives one or more of his christian names in full. Unless previous entries are altered, one may have several variations, *e.g.* F. B. Young, Francis B. Young, and Francis Brett Young.

The cards will be arranged in the catalogue according to surnames, so these are given first in headings. To help the filer, the "key-word" should be put in block capitals. Then comes a comma, the christian names, and a full stop punctuation mark.

e.g. PLOMER, Henry Ralph.

If the christian names cannot be found, then leave a space of two centimetres between each initial for the name to be added later. In this case do not put a full stop after the initial. Thus a title-page reading *Bookbinding | by | S. T. Prideaux* will have the catalogue entry heading,

PRIDEAUX, S   T

As a rule titles like *Reverend, Canon, General,* can be ignored. These, together with degrees and descriptions, such as *of the British Museum,* are only put in the heading when required to separate authors who have identical names, e.g. William Brown, *M.A.* and William Brown, *antiquarian.*

4. TRANSCRIBING THE TITLE

The A.A. code gives the following definition of title:
1. In the broad sense, the distinguishing name of any written production as given on the title-page, including the name of the author, editor, translator, the edition, etc., but excluding the imprint.
2. In the narrow sense the title does not include the name of the author, editor, etc.

Should the cataloguer interpret the term in its broad or narrow sense when transcribing the title for a catalogue entry? In printed catalogues, titles are usually shortened because of high printing costs, but this is not necessary in a written or typed card catalogue. Here omissions should usually be limited to such extra matter as mottoes, quotations, particulars of author's qualifications or previous works. The author's name must be repeated and given in the exact form in which it appears in the title, although this may differ from the heading. Details about the author are kept for special notes at the end of the entry, provided these facts are important, although designations preceding the name, *e.g. Rev., Major*, are usually copied in the title. A statement of the number of illustrations, or the series to which a work belongs, are also omitted, as these have a place further on in the entry.

The following example shows material that may be left out. The sign / denotes the end of a line on the title-page.

THE / BOY'S COUNTRY-BOOK. / BY / WILLIAM HOWITT, / AUTHOR OF "THE RURAL LIFE OF ENGLAND," "VISITS TO / REMARKABLE PLACES," / ETC. / "AWAY THEY SCAMPER FULL OF SPORT AWAY, / WITH CARELESS MINDS INTENT ON VARIOUS PLAY; / HUZZA!—A LONG AND SUNNY HOLYDAY! / SOME, THE PROJECTED RACING-MATCH DECIDE; / etc. The quotation continues for another four lines, but all the cataloguer need copy in an entry is, *The boy's country-book, by William Howitt* . . . The three dots show that something has been omitted.

Beginners should be careful not to omit essential title matter. For example, *Account / of the / Russian Discoveries / between / Asia and America. / To which are added, / The Conquest of Siberia, and / The History / of the / Transactions and Commerce / between / Russia and China. / By / William Coxe, A.M. F.R.S. F.S.A. / Canon Residentiary of Sarum, and / Rector of Bemerton. / The Fourth Edition, considerably enlarged.* Only the author's degrees and titles following his name should be omitted.

Edition is considered part of the title and must be included, also such descriptions as *revised*, or *greatly enlarged* as well as the actual number. Readers often require a certain edition, which alone will serve their purpose. They also find it useful to know if a new edition is a real revision of the work, not merely a reprint with a few minor additions. Title-page statements are sometimes misleading, but the information is helpful at times and worth including. *Impression, issue, reprint*, do not cover changes in the text, so need not be mentioned.

As far as is practical, the title-page's punctuation should be followed, but the cataloguer may supply his own punctuation when necessary. No attempt is made to reproduce title-page capitalization. Capitals only confuse the eye and make the catalogue difficult to read, so their use is kept down to the absolute minimum.

Before beginning to transcribe a title, the student should learn Rules 136, 172, and 148 of the A.A. code. For convenience they are given here.

136 The title is usually to be given in full, including the author's name, and is to be an exact transcript of the title-page, except that mottoes and non-essential matter of any kind, as well as designation of series, may be omitted, the omissions being indicated by three dots (. . .). The punctuation of the title-page is generally to be followed; if there is no punctuation it is to be supplied.

172 Initial capital letters are to be used for names of persons, personifications, places, and bodies, for substitutes for proper names, and for adjectives derived from these names; for the first word of the title of a book. . . . In all doubtful cases avoid the use of capitals. In foreign languages follow the local practice.

148 Consider the statement specifying the edition as a part of the title. It is to be given in the language of the book and in the order of the title-page . . .

Begin the title at the second of the two margins, but when starting the second and subsequent lines, begin at the first margin (*see* Example 2, page 26).

Often a long title consists of title proper and a subsidiary, explanatory phrase, which is called the sub-title. If the cataloguer is supplying the punctuation, he separates the two by a colon.

e.g. Glimpses of four continents: letters written during a tour in Australia, New Zealand, and North America, in 1893.

An alternative title is one introduced by *or*. The book may be referred to by this title, so it should always be given. Here, a semicolon marks off the title proper.

e.g. Microscopical praxis; or, Simple methods of ascertaining the properties of various microscopical accessories.

The first word of an alternative title begins with a capital letter.

5. THE IMPRINT

Place of publication, publisher's name, and date of publication make up the imprint. These items are usually found at the bottom of the title-page, but may be on the back, especially the date. They are given in the same paragraph as the title, but, for the sake of clearness, a space of two centimetres should be left. The order of the items is place, name, date, and each is separated from the next by a comma. The publisher's address need not be given, and a very long publisher's name may be abbreviated (*see* Example 3, page 27).

Sometimes there are two places of publication. In that case, the first should be chosen, unless it is definitely known that the second is more important. For example, *Cassell and Company, Ltd., London, Toronto, Melbourne and Sydney* should be given as *London, Cassell and Company, Ltd.*

If there are two or more places and two or more publishers, give the first unless a subsequent one is the chief. The same practice is followed if there is one place, but two or more publishers.

The date is always given in arabic figures. If there is no date, then it should be found or an approximate one estimated. A date taken from any source other than the title-page (front or back) must be put in square brackets. A doubtful item is followed by an interrogation mark, *e.g.* [1905?].

A.A. rules 150, 152, 155, and 156 cover imprint.

150 After the title give the place or places . . . of publication in the language of the title.

152 After the name of the place give the name of the publisher in the language of the title . . .

155 Give the date found on the title-page, in arabic figures . . .

156 When there is no imprint date the year of publication, if it can be ascertained, is to be given in brackets, and if uncertain, to be given approximately . . .

6. THE COLLATION

The collation consists of the number of pages in a single volume, or number of volumes if more than one; specification of illustrations; and height of the book. These items, together with statement of series, form the second paragraph of a catalogue entry.

The value to readers of this information is sometimes queried. Early printed books have special cataloguing rules, since one copy may differ from another and great collation detail is needed. But books printed after 1500 are "modern" and, except for occasional rare bibliographical specimens, the purpose of collation is only to draw the reader's attention to certain physical features which may help him in selecting a work from the catalogue. This is especially important in a closed library, but in an open-access library he may wish to reserve a book that has been loaned to someone else. Thus it is useful to have information about the number of volumes. Even if the work consists of a single volume, the reader may like to know whether it consists of a thousand-odd pages, or is a mere pamphlet. He may require an illustrated rather than an unillustrated copy, an historical book that contains maps and portraits, or a technical work with diagrams. Height is important in showing if a work is unduly small or large, or an otherwise unusual shape. Cross measurements are given as well in the latter instance. Certainly this item of the collation might be omitted for average-sized books, but the A.A. code prescribes its inclusion in the catalogue entry for all cases. Some British libraries measure in inches, not centimetres.

The A.A. collation rules are as follows:—

158 Give all items of collation in English and in the following order: 1st, volumes or pages; 2nd, illustrations; 3rd, size.

159 Give the number of volumes, or of pages if there is only one volume.

160 Indicate the number of pages by giving the last number of each paging, separating the numbers by a comma. The addition of unpaged matter may be shown by a +, or the number of pages, ascertained by counting, may be given in brackets. Give paging in arabic or roman figures, according to the book. In unpaged works, and in works having the pages lettered, or numbered in figures other than arabic or roman (*e.g.* Greek) the number of pages may be given in brackets, the signatures being noted only in the case of rare and important works.

161 Give illustrations in the following order: frontispiece, illustrations, plates, photographs, portraits, maps, plans, facsimiles, tables, diagrams.

Give the number of plates, maps, etc., when it can be easily ascertained.

Plates, portraits, etc., are to be specified whether included in the paging or not.

164 Give height of book in centimetres, exact to one-half centimetre. . . . When books are "narrow," "square," "oblong," or otherwise of very unusual size, give both dimensions . . .

When applying these rules, the student must first ascertain

how many volumes the work occupies. If more than one, he states 2v., or whatever the number. Volumes I and II bound together are described as 2v. in 1. It should be noted that the collation interpretation of *volume* is "whatever is contained in one binding." A work may be divided into several volumes, each with its own title-page, but if the library only possesses one of these, *e.g.* Volume III, then that will be a single volume for purposes of collation.

The number of pages must be given for a single volume, and here the beginner encounters difficulties owing to publishers' varied methods of counting pages. The end-papers are always ignored, but the publisher may include half-title, title-page, preface, contents table, as well as actual text and index, in the total. This figure may be an odd or an even number, according to whether printing ends on the recto or the verso side of a leaf. It is more usual for the publisher to count the preliminary pages (*i.e.* those before the beginning of the actual text) in roman numerals, and the text in arabic. Only part of the preliminary pages may be numbered, sometimes none at all.

Here are some examples of different numberings.

(1) Half-title page to end of text with arabic figures 1 to 379. The verso side of the last leaf is blank and unnumbered. There are sixteen pages of advertising matter (a publisher's catalogue) and these are numbered 1 to 16.

(2) Half-title page to end of preliminary matter in roman figures i to xii, text in arabic 1 to 367.

(3) Half-title page to end of preliminary matter unnumbered. Three of the pages have printed matter on one side only, the other side being blank. Text 1 to 367.

(4) Half-title page and title-page unnumbered. Rest of preliminary matter numbered i to viii. Text 1 to 367.

(5) Preliminary pages numbered i to xi, but verso side of last leaf unnumbered. Text 1 to 367.

(6) First eight preliminary pages numbered i to viii, last four unnumbered. Text 1 to 367.

The paging in each case would be expressed as follows:—

(1) 379p. In this case, accept the publisher's numbering and ignore the final blank page. The advertising matter is not really part of the book and is never included.

(2) xii,367p.

(3) [xii],367p. Ignore blanks. Put your figure in square brackets. Use roman to indicate preliminary paging.

(4) [iv]viii,367p.

(5) xi,367p. No need to explain blank. Its presence is obvious, as it is on the verso side of a leaf.

(6) viii[iv],367p.

The A.A. rule allows unpaged matter to be shown by a plus sign, or counted and put in square brackets. The second method should be followed.

The purpose in giving pagination for modern books is only to indicate the volume's bulk, so unnecessary elaboration must be avoided. There is no need to specify blanks. When the cataloguer supplies the number of pages, he should use roman figures for preliminary matter and arabic for text, separating the two by a comma. This distinguishes them and saves the confusing abbreviation *p.l.* used by the Library of Congress.

According to the A.A. code, illustrations* must be given in detail. Certainly the mere description *illustrated* is meaningless to a student who requires maps or facsimiles. Abbreviations may be used. These, and definitions of some of the terms, are set out below.

Frontispiece.—A plate or other illustration facing (or preceding) the title-page. Abbreviated to *front.* or *fronts.*

Illustration.—In a narrow sense the term stands for illustrations in the text. Abbreviated to *illus.*

* The term used is in a broad sense. (*See* A.A. definition.)

Plates.—A full-page illustration usually printed on special (heavy) paper, one side of the leaf being blank. Plates are not as a rule included in the paging. Abbreviated to *pl.* in the singular, but no abbreviation for the plural.

Abbreviations for the other kind of illustrations are: phot., photos., port., ports., facsim., facsims., tab. (in plural tables), diagr., diagrs. No abbreviation is used for map or plan.

Plates, etc., need only be counted when necessary for checking (*e.g.* in a book that contains fine artistic illustrations). The number may also be given when it is considered really useful to the reader and is easily ascertained from the contents table or list of illustrations. The fact that any are coloured or folded need not be mentioned.

It should be noted that a frontispiece is also a plate and may, in addition, be a map, or portrait, or facsimile, or photograph, etc. Portraits, photographs, etc., are often on plates. To add to the difficulties, the title-page description of illustrations may be quite different from that description in accordance with A.A. rules. A title-page states, "With over thirty illustrations," and, on examination, these turn out to be frontispiece, plates, and two maps, but no illustrations set in the text. In another instance, "Numerous photographs and diagrams" consist of a frontispiece, three coloured plates that are also photographs, and several diagrammatic text illustrations. A third title-page specifies "Thirty-two plates," of which one is a frontispiece and twenty-eight of the remainder are portraits.

Obviously the cataloguer must ignore the publisher's description of illustrative matter and follow the A.A. code conventions. A supplementary rule of the Library of Congress is useful here in indicating the precedence of frontispiece over other types of illustrations, and showing when these must also be designated. "Any illustration, other than an engraved title, facing or immediately preceding the title-page, shall be designated in the collation as a frontispiece, thus: front., front.(port), front.(map), *but not* front.(pl.). When the book contains other illustrations of the same character the specification after 'front' is to be omitted." The same ruling should be followed for portraits, facsimiles, etc., that are also plates and often photographs. Simply describe them as ports. or facsims.

Do not use capitals for the words front., illus., etc. A comma should separate each item, and the actual enumeration of illustrations follow one centimetre after the items of pagination. Pagination, or number of volumes, begins at the inner margin, on a fresh line below the imprint (*see* Example 4, page 27).

Size, as expressed by height, must be distinguished from the format given for early printed books. Format concerns the folding of the paper. When paper sizes were fairly uniform, a sheet folded once produced a book thirty centimetres high, or over, and this was called a folio. Similarly, the quarto was a book between twenty-five and thirty centimetres high and had the original sheets of paper folded twice, each sheet producing four leaves. Some libraries use these terms for oversize books, irrespective of format, but actual measurement for modern books is more satisfactory. Paper sizes are now so varied that a book twenty-five centimetres high is not necessarily the product of two foldings.

The measurement should be taken from the cover, not the title-page. Only height need be given unless the book is unusual in other respects. Leave a space of one centimetre after the illustration items, *e.g.* vii,352p. front., plates, ports. 23cm.

7. SERIES

Series may be defined as "a number of separate works, usually related to one another in subject or otherwise, issued in succession, normally by the same publisher and in uniform style, with a collective title which generally appears at the head of the title-page, on the half-title, or on the cover."

Rule 166 says that the series should be given in parenthesis after the collation. When it appears at the top of the title-page, it is omitted from the actual title. The volume number should be included, but such details as editor, source (*e.g.* half-title page, cover), may be omitted. Leave a space of two centimetres after statement of size and continue with the series in the same paragraph (*see* Example 5, page 28).

8. Examples

(*a*) Initials, not full christian names on title-page, and military title to be omitted in heading. Guns and Cavalry / Their Performances in the Past / and their Prospects in the Future / by / Major E. S. May, R.A. / author of "Achievements of Field Artillery" / with Plans and Illustrations / London, / Sampson Low, Marston and Company / Limited / St. Dunstan's House / Fetter Lane, Fleet Street, E.C. / 1896 /.

There are ten numbered preliminary pages, two unnumbered, and two hundred and twenty of text. There are twelve portraits, including the frontispiece, three plates, and four plans. Height is nineteen centimetres (*see* Example 6, page 28).

(*b*) Omission from beginning of title. Edition stated, but place in square brackets to show that cataloguer has put it out of title-page sequence. Date in square brackets because supplied from source other than title-page. Omission of advertising matter. Third Edition. Fifteenth Thousand. / Practical / Hydropathy. / Including / Plans of Baths, / and Remarks on / Diet, Clothing, and Habits of Life. / By John Smedley, / Lea Mills, Derby. / With One Hundred and Sixty Anatomical Engravings, / and Physiological Explanations, / Plans of Baths, etc. / Price Two

SHILLINGS AND SIXPENCE. / OR FREE PER POST FOR 36 POSTAGE STAMPS / OF THE AUTHOR OR BOOKSELLER. / LONDON, / PARTRIDGE AND CO., PATERNOSTER ROW, / AND ALL BOOKSELLERS. / Introduction bears the date 1858. Pages are numbered i to xiv, 15 to 512. There are four pages of advertising matter for Matlock Bank Hydropathic Establishment. There are illustrations, plans and diagrams set in the text. The height of the book is nineteen centimetres (*see* Example 7, page 29).

(*c*) Belongs to a series. Initials only on title-page. No illustrations. THE / ARIAN CONTROVERSY. / BY / H. M. GWATKIN, M.A. / LECTURER AND LATE FELLOW OF ST. JOHN'S COLLEGE, / CAMBRIDGE. / LONDON, / LONGMANS, GREEN, AND CO. / 1889. / All rights reserved /. There are eleven numbered preliminary pages, one hundred and seventy-six of text, and a publisher's catalogue of sixteen pages. Height of the book is eighteen centimetres. On the half-title page is *Epochs of Church History* / EDITED BY / PROFESSOR MANDELL CREIGHTON. / THE ARIAN CONTROVERSY / (*see* Example 8, page 29).

(*d*) Work in two volumes. Date given in roman figures, so must be put into arabic. PRINCIPLES / OF / POLITICAL ECONOMY / WITH / SOME OF THEIR APPLICATIONS TO SOCIAL PHILOSOPHY. / BY / JOHN STUART MILL. / IN TWO VOLUMES. / VOL. I / FOURTH EDITION. / LONDON, / JOHN W. PARKER AND SON, WEST STRAND. / M.DCCC.LVII. / The title-page of Volume II is the same, except for the statement VOL. II. Both volumes are twenty-three centimetres high, and there are no illustrations, neither do they belong to a series (*see* Example 9, page 30).

Note: A location symbol (usually the classification and author marks combined) and an accession number are often given on the catalogue card. As these are not cataloguing items and their use varies in different libraries, they are not included in the examples given in this book.

1

Standard catalogue card showing ruling of headline and margins.

2

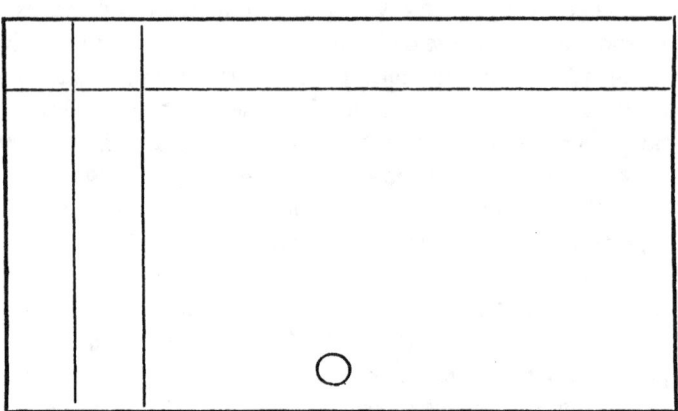

ROUT	H, Edward John.
the	An elementary treatise on dynamics of a system of
rigi	d bodies, with numerous
exam	ples, by Edward John
Rout	h. Third edition, revised
and	enlarged.

Method of setting out title.

3

TWO YEARS ON THE ALABAMA / BY / ARTHUR SINCLAIR / LIEUTENANT, C.S.N. / WITH OVER THIRTY ILLUSTRATIONS / LONDON / GAY AND BIRD, PUBLISHERS / 22 BEDFORD STREET, STRAND / 1896.

	SINC	LAIR, Arthur.
		Two years on the Alabama, by Arthur Sinclair... London, Gay and Bird, 1896.

Method of setting out imprint.

4

	DOUG	HTY, Henry Montagu.
		Our wherry in Wendish lands: from Friesland through the Mecklenburg Lakes to Bohemia: By H.M. Doughty... London, Jarrold & Sons, [189–?] 406p. front., illus., plates, maps.

Setting out and punctuation of collation details.

5

	YOUNG, Charles Augustus.	
		The sun, by C.A.Young... Second edition. London, Kegan Paul,Trench, & Co.,1883. 321p. front., illus., pl., diagrs. 19cm. (The international scientific series, v. XXXIX.)

Method of setting out series title.

6

	MAY, Edward Sinclair.	
		Guns and cavalry: their performances in the past and their prospects in the future, by Major E.S.May... London, Sampson Low, Marston and Company Limited, 1896. x[ii],220p. front., plates, ports., plans. 19cm.

Specimen author entry.

7

SMEDLEY, John.	
	... Practical hydropathy: including...remarks on diet, clothing, and habits of life. By John Smedley...[Third edition]. London, Partridge and Co. [1858]. 512p. illus., plans, diagrs. 19cm.

Specimen author entry.

8

GWATKIN, Henry Melvill.	
	The Arian controversy. By H.M. Gwatkin... London, Longmans, Green, and Co., 1889. xi,176p. 18cm. (Epochs of church history)

Specimen author entry.

9

	MILL, John Stuart.
	Principles of political economy, with some of their applications to social philosophy. By John Stuart Mill. In two volumes... Fourth edition. London, John W. Parker and Son, 1857. 2v. 23cm.

Specimen author entry.

CHAPTER II

AUTHOR AND TITLE ADDED ENTRIES

1. KINDS OF ENTRY

CHAPTER I only dealt with the single author main entry, that is, the one made under the name of an individual. A main entry is the chief entry for a book and is most commonly made under the person who is principally, if not entirely, responsible for its existence.

Other people may have helped, although they are not actually authors. For example, there is the person who edits, or abridges, or revises, or translates someone else's work. A second, or, as it is technically called, added entry is made under his name. When two authors or more collaborate, all except the first are regarded as subsidiary and given added entries. Rules 2 to 22 of the Anglo-American code are mainly concerned with such instances.

2. UNIT CARDS

Before the use of printed unit cards became general in the U.S.A., the main entry was detailed (as described in Chapter I), but the added entry only gave a shortened title and omitted all, or part, of the imprint and collation. This practice is still followed in many British libraries.

In the unit card system, an exact copy of the main entry is used for the added entry, and the extra heading added above the original one. Students are instructed here to follow that method.

The following example requires the two kinds of entry, a main for the author proper, and an added for the editor.

FUNGI: THEIR NATURE / INFLUENCE, AND USES / BY / M. C.

COOKE, M.A., LL.D. / EDITED BY THE REV. M. J. BERKELEY, M.A., F.L.S. / THIRD EDITION / LONDON / KEGAN PAUL, TRENCH & CO., 1 PATERNOSTER SQUARE / 1883 /. There are twelve roman numbered preliminary and two hundred and ninety-nine arabic numbered text pages, with a publisher's catalogue of forty-four pages bound in at the end. Illustrations are set in the text. The book is nineteen centimetres high. The half-title page reads, THE INTERNATIONAL SCIENTIFIC SERIES / VOLUME XIV (*see* Examples 10 and 11, page 38).

It will be seen that the two cards are identical, except for the extra heading of editor's name in the added entry. This heading must be placed within the second margin to show the secondary nature of the entry. The abbreviation *ed.* is placed after the name and printed in italics. In a written or typed catalogue, it is underlined.

This set-out makes filing of cards much easier. Supposing that Miles Joseph Berkeley has edited several books, all by different authors. When filing these added entries under his name in the catalogue it will be quite simple to sub-arrange them alphabetically by authors edited.

The main entry card should also carry a record of all added entries that have been made for that book. This is very important for future alterations, or even withdrawals. Perhaps the cataloguer could not discover the full name of M. C. Cooke at the time of cataloguing, but found it when a later work was published. He would fill in the blanks left in the main entry heading, but without a note of the added entry he might overlook the second heading in the Berkeley card. These tracings, as they are called, enable a cataloguer to check all other cards pertaining to a book. As the record is only for staff use, it is brief and usually made on the back of the card, so as not to be confused with entry details (*see* Example 12, page 39).

3. STRAIGHTFORWARD RULES FOR AUTHOR ADDED ENTRY

The simplest rules in the first section of the A.A. code are Nos. 21, 17, and 18. They cover translators; epitomizers, *i.e.* those who abridge or summarize larger works, while keeping the essential matter of the original; and compilers of extracts, selections, and chrestomathies (choice passages). In every case, main entry is made under the author of the original work, and added entry under the translator, etc. After a translator's name the abbreviation *tr.* is added in the heading. *Ed.* or *comp.* serves for the others. Editorial work usually involves explanatory notes, or revision of text as is necessary when making an abridgement. The compiler merely collects the printed material from different sources.

The set-out for these added entries is the same as that given for the previous example (*see* Example 13, page 39).

4. RULES WHERE A DECISION MUST BE MADE

Three important rules where a decision is necessary are No. 4 (Illustrators), No. 13 (Commentaries), and No. 19 (Revisions). Here the question, "Under whom as author" has to be considered.

Rule 4 prescribes added entry under the illustrator, provided the illustrations are subsidiary to the text. If the book consists solely of illustrations, or if these are the chief feature and more important than the text, the position is reversed. Main entry is then made under the illustrator and added entry under writer of the text. The cataloguer has to decide which is the more important. In cases of doubt, main entry is made under the author of the text.

The same principle is applied to commentaries, Rule 13. If the original text is given, then main entry is made under the author of that text, and the commentator has an added entry.

Main entry is made under the latter when the original text is broken up, or printed in small type, or its subordinate position indicated in some other way. The author of the original text then has an added entry.

If a revision has become a completely new work with little of the original left, then the reviser has a main entry and the original author an added entry. But often the reviser's work is more akin to that of an editor, or he may only have rewritten one or two chapters. The original author's name will still occupy the chief position on the title-page. For example, *Practical anatomy: a manual of dissections, by Christopher Heath . . . Sixth edition, revised by Rickman J. Godlee* . . . This is obviously a case where main entry will be made under Heath, and added entry under Godlee.

The abbreviations used in the heading are *illus*. for illustrator, *ed*. for commentator. Nothing is added after a reviser's name.

5. JOINT AUTHORS

Rule 2 (Joint authors) orders a variation from the ordinary heading, which so far has only consisted of one name. The rule is as follows: "Enter a work written jointly by two authors (including correspondence) under the name of the one first mentioned on the title-page, followed by the name of the second, in the form Besant, *Sir* Walter, *and* Rice, James . . ." The Library of Congress only gives the name of the first author, and in the 1941 American revised edition of the A.A. this practice is followed. The amended rule reads: "Enter under the first author mentioned on the title-page a work produced jointly by two or more authors in which the contribution of each is not a separate and distinct part of the whole."

This is the more sensible method and it avoids a long, cumbersome heading. British libraries, however, are so used to the older form for two authors that the student is advised to keep to that. Added entry must be made under the second author.

The word *and* is underlined because it is ignored in filing. If printed, it should appear in italics (*see* Examples 14 and 15, pages 39 and 40).

Rule 2 (in the 1908 edition) continues: "When there are more than two authors use the form Doe, John, *and others*; give the name of the others in the title if there are no more than three, or if more than three, in a note or in the contents. Make added entries . . . for the second and following authors." (*see* Example 16, page 40).

One does not often have instances of more than three authors collaborating. Several people may have contributed chapters, but there will be an editor responsible for the book as a whole. Unless there is real collaboration for the entire work, Rule 2 does not apply and such composite publications will be considered in a later chapter.

Here is a case where the authors have apparently worked together for production of the whole book, *Political thought: the European tradition. By J. P. Mayer in co-operation with R. H. S. Crossman, P. Kecskemeti, E. Kohn-Bramstedt, C. J. S. Sprigge.* The names of these four secondary authors will be omitted from the title, but given in a note below the catalogue entry. (For notes and contents, see Chapter VI.)

6. OTHER AUTHOR ADDED ENTRY RULES

The student should now study the remainder of Rules 2 to 22. Some of these, such as old dissertations, heraldic visitations, papal bulls, and manuscripts, are seldom used by the average cataloguer. Rule 6 deals with maps and Rules 8 to 10 with musical compositions, librettos and thematic catalogues. Rule 16 (Concordances) is one of the eight alternative rules where each Association has made a different decision. The British method should be followed by students in this country.

The second part of Rule 12 (Bulls) orders reference, not added entry, from name of pope. Rule 14 (Continuations, *i.e.* Supplements) directs the same from author of the original work when entry is made under author of the continuation. This is not an entry, but a special kind of direction, called the *see also* reference. It should be set out as follows:—

The heading begins at the inner margin, so the title has to be indented a further centimetre. The words *see also* are indented yet another centimetre and are underlined. The names of authors, to whom reference is made, begin at the first margin (*see* Example 17, page 41).

Rules 2, 13, 18, 19 allow references as alternatives to added entries. The student should not take any notice of these, but make added entries. Added entries are more in keeping with the rest of the section. They are also more useful, in these cases, for a large, or moderately large, catalogue.

7. TITLE ADDED ENTRY

In an Author-title, or a Dictionary, catalogue, added entry under the title of a book is often made. Part of Rule 169 states: ". . . Make added entries for the titles of all novels and plays and of poems likely to be remembered by their titles; for other striking titles . . ." A reader will often ask for a book by title when he has forgotten the author.

It is waste of time to make title entry when the subject is obvious, since such books can be traced in the subject catalogue. It is easy to guess where to find *Eskimoland speaks, I planted trees, We saw the holy city,* even when the author's name is not known. A still more absurd practice is to fill the catalogue with title entries beginning *Textbook, Manual,* and such commonly used words.

As the rule indicates, added title entry should only be made for works of pure literature, *e.g. Euphues, All for love, The dynasts, Moonlight is silver*; and for striking titles generally, *e.g. Anna and the king of Siam, In love with life, The Queen thanks Sir Howard.*

In title entry, the first word, not an article, is taken as the catch-word, *e.g.* EUPHUES, ALL, DYNASTS, MOONLIGHT, ANNA, IN, QUEEN. Only *a, an, the,* and their foreign equivalents are disregarded at the beginning. Libraries do modify this rule with certain titles, where the most important word comes later, but the student should apply it strictly. He should also adopt the same style for title added entries as for author ones, that is, use the key-word only for heading (*see* Example 18, page 41).

8. AUTHOR AND TITLE ADDED ENTRIES, ALSO TRACING
(*see* Examples 19 to 22, pages 42–3).

The cataloguer, who is working in a library, will probably be allowed to exercise his own discretion about added entries. Much depends on the nature of the library, but, for example, it is not usually worth while to make these for little-known illustrators, especially if their work be slight. The cataloguing student, however, is not applying the rules in a library. He is not affected by custom and individual needs, therefore he must follow the A.A. code with absolute fidelity and make all the entries prescribed, whether they seem to him to be important or otherwise.

EXAMPLES

10

	COOK	E, Mordecai Cubitt.
		Fungi: their nature, influence, and uses, by M.C. Cooke... edited by the Rev. M.J. Berkeley... Third edition.　　London, Kegan Paul, Trench and Co., 1883. 　　xii,299p.　illus.　19cm. (The international scientific series, v.XIV)

Main entry.

11

		BERKELEY, Miles Joseph, ed.
	COOK	E, Mordecai Cubitt.
		Fungi: their nature, influence, and uses, by M.C. Cooke... edited by the Rev. M.J. Berkeley... Third edition.　　London, Kegan Paul, Trench and Co., 1883. 　　xii,299p.　illus.　19cm. (The international scientific series, v.XIV)

Added entry.

12

Added entries
BERKELEY, Miles Joseph, ed.

Back of main entry card.

13

WHITE, Maude Valérie, tr.
MUNTHE, Axel.
　　Letters from a mourning city (Naples, autumn, 1884), by Axel Munthe; translated from the Swedish, by Maude Valérie White.　　London, John Murray, 1887.
　　vii,289p.　front.　19cm.

Added entry.

14

COHEN, Morris R　　, and Nagel, Ernest.
　　An introduction to logic and scientific method, by Morris R. Cohen... and Ernest Nagel...　　London, George Routledge and Sons, Ltd., 1934.
　　xii,467p.　21½cm.

Main entry.

15

	NAGEL, Ernest, jt. author.
	COHEN, Morris R , and
	Nagel, Ernest. An introduction to logic and scientific method, by Morris R. Cohen... and Ernest Nagel... London, George Routledge and Sons, Ltd., 1934. xii,467p. 21½cm.

Added entry.

16

	WILSON, P G , and others.
	La vie commerciale: an introduction to commercial French covering all the usual operations of a business house and commercial correspondence, by P.G.Wilson... Fernand Herbert... and Jean Herbert... London, Sir Isaac Pitman and Sons, Ltd., 1934. xiv,175p. map. 18½cm.

Example for three authors.

17

		HAIN, Ludwig Friedrich Theodor.
		Repertorium biblio-graphicum <u>see also</u>
	COPI	NGER, Walter Arthur. Supplement to Hain's Repertorium biblio-graphicum.
	REIC	HLING, Dietrich. Appendices ad Hainii-Copingeri Repertorium biblio-graphicum.

See also reference.

18

		CRUISE
	STAB	LES, Gordon.
		The cruise of the land yacht ''Wanderer''; or, Thirteen hundred miles in my caravan, by Gordon Stables... London, Hodder and Stoughton, 1886.
		xii,351p. front., illus. 22cm.

Added title entry.

19

	BOYD	, Mary Stuart.
		Our stolen summer: the record of a roundabout tour, by Mary Stuart Boyd. With... sketches by A.S.Boyd. London, William Blackwood and Sons,1900.
		xiv,392p.　illus.　23½cm.

Main entry.

20

		BOYD, A　　S　　,illus.
	BOYD	, Mary Stuart.
		Our stolen summer: the record of a roundabout tour, by Mary Stuart Boyd. With... sketches by A.S.Boyd. London, William Blackwood and Sons,1900.
		xiv,392p.　illus.　23½cm.

Added author entry.

21

```
|      |OUR                          |
|BOYD  |, Mary Stuart.               |
|------|-----------------------------|
|      |Our stolen summer: the       |
|reco  |rd of a roundabout tour,     |
|by M  |ary Stuart Boyd.  With...    |
|sket  |ches by A.S.Boyd.            |
|Lond  |on, William Blackwood and    |
|Sons  |, 1900.                      |
|      |xiv,392p.  illus.  23½cm.    |
```

Added title entry.

22

Added entries
BOYD, A   S   , illus.
OUR

Tracing on back of main entry.

CHAPTER III

AUTHOR REFERENCES

1. WHAT IS MEANT BY A REFERENCE?

THE A.A. code defines *entry* as "The record of a book in a catalogue or list," and *reference* as "A direction from one heading to another." References in a catalogue are signposts. They either warn one away from a particular spot, or they guide one to similar places.

The *see* reference is like the "No thoroughfare" or "Please keep off the grass" signs. A heading that is not to be used for catalogue entries has a *see* reference under it to direct readers to the correct heading. The word *see* connects the two. This type of reference is more common in author cataloguing, and is used throughout the next section of the A.A. code, which is entitled, "Under what part or form of name."

The other type of reference is called the *see also* and is rare in author cataloguing. It shows a reader that although a particular heading is already used for entry purposes, yet further information can be obtained under another heading. Its function was demonstrated in Chapter II, section 6, with an example of a continuation, or supplement, to another work. Here, the original work is entered under its own author, Hain, and the continuations under Copinger and Reichling respectively. In addition, a *see also* reference is made under Hain, telling the reader to try the headings for Copinger and for Reichling as well. A *see* reference would have been wrong here because there already is a catalogue entry under Hain.

The *see* reference means, "Nothing here. Look elsewhere."

The *see also* means, "For further information, look somewhere else."

Rules 23 to 57 are only concerned with *see* references.

2. GENERAL RULES

Two rules affect the entire section that deals with the problem of choosing one form, or one part, of an individual author's name. Rule 23 states, "In the heading give names of authors in full and in their vernacular form, with certain specified exceptions. . . . Refer from the form not adopted." Rule 57 explains, "The names of editors, translators, continuators, etc., are subject to the same rules as the names of authors."

3. ENTRY OF SURNAMES AND FORENAMES

The use of surnames did not become common until the fourteenth century, so the cataloguer is obliged to enter earlier authors under their forenames. Sovereigns, popes, and (according to the British alternative rule) princes of the blood are still catalogued in the same way (Rules 31, 32, 45 to 48). A prince of the blood, *i.e.* member of a royal house, is given a reference from any title, or titles, that he may possess.

This reference is set out as below. The heading begins at the inner margin. If continued on a second line, it again starts there. The *see* is put on a line below the heading and indented one centimetre further to the right. The heading to which reference is made starts at the first margin. Only the first word of each heading is put in block capitals (*see* Example 23, page 55). The word *see*; titles; and descriptions of titles, *e.g. of Clarence and Avondale;* when they follow the names, are all underlined and appear in italics if printed.

Andrew Maunsell, in 1595, was the first to arrange an author catalogue by surnames, not forenames. In 1601, Sir Thomas Bodley was complaining to the first Bodley's librarian, "Againe I did alwaies wishe that in the setting downe of an Autours title, yow would place his surname first." From the seventeenth century this has been the established cataloguing practice.

Except for authors who do not possess a surname or, as in the case of Popes, are no longer known by it, entry is made under surname, with the forenames following. This is covered by Rule 24.

Rules 27 to 30 deal with varied forms of forenames, also compound and unused ones. The rule for unused forenames is the most important. "Omit forenames not used by the author and not represented by initials on the title-pages of his works." Thus, Hilaire Belloc is entered as BELLOC, Hilaire, not BELLOC, Joseph Hilaire Pierre. But title-pages give H. G. Wells, so the names represented by initials can be supplied and he will be entered as WELLS, Herbert George.

Rule 37 provides for distinguishing people of the same name by the addition of birth and death dates, or descriptive designations. It is preferable to use the former. This practice really depends on the size of the catalogue. It is not often necessary in the average library, except for common names like John Jones and William Brown.

4. DIFFICULT SURNAMES

Surnames like Howard, Johnson, Walker, present no difficulty, but many authors have a compound surname. This may consist of two surnames joined by a hyphen, *e.g.* Kaye-Smith; a preposition, or article, and surname, *e.g.* De Morgan, Le Sage; or a long combination made up of father's and mother's surnames and an estate name, *e.g.* Alcala Zamora y Torres.

Rule 25 orders compound surnames to be entered under the first part of the name, with references from the other parts. Occasional exceptions are permitted if custom has favoured entry under some other part. For example, the French writer, Fenelon, has never been known as Salignac de La Mothe-Fenelon. But *Some masters of Spanish verse,* by James Fitzmaurice-Kelly, would have as entry heading, FITZMAURICE-KELLY, James (*see* Example 24, page 56).

Surnames with prefixes (Rule 26) are entered under the part following the prefix, but there are four important exceptions. These are: "(*a*) in English; (*b*) in French when the prefix consists of or contains an article; (*c*) in Italian and Spanish when the prefix consists simply of an article; (*d*) when the prefix and the name are written as one word."

Examples. (N.B.—All parts of a compound surname should be put in block capitals in the heading.)

Hyphenated surname.	GROSE-HODGE, Humfrey. Refer from HODGE, Humfrey Grose-.
Foreign, non-hyphenated surname.	ÁLVAREZ QUINTERO, Serafín. Refer from QUINTERO, Serafín Álvarez.
Surname with prefix.	MUSSET, Alfred de. Refer from DE MUSSET, Alfred.
	ESSEN, Gerhardus van. Refer from VAN ESSEN, Gerhardus.

Exceptions to Prefix Rule

English (and American).	DE QUINCEY, Thomas. Refer from QUINCEY, Thomas de.
	VAN VALIN, W. B. Refer from VALIN, W. B. van.
French, when prefix consists of or contains an article.	DU BELLAY, Joachim. Refer from BELLAY, Joachim du.
	LA TOUCHE, N. de. Refer from DE LA TOUCHE, N. and TOUCHE, N. de la.
	LE CLERCQ, Chrétien. Refer from CLERCQ, Chrétien le.
Italian and Spanish (including Portuguese and Latin-American). When prefix consists only of an article.	LO VECCHIO MUSTI, M. Refer from VECCHIO MUSTI, M. and MUSTI, M. Lo Vecchio.
	LA PIANA, A. Refer from PIANA, A. la.
Prefix compounded with surname.	DELISLE, Léopold Victor. No reference.
	VANHÖFFEN, Ernst. No reference.

The student must beware of certain pitfalls in compound names. Spanish ones are particularly difficult. English surnames are not considered compound unless they consist of prefix and name, or two names joined by a hyphen. Thus, Du Maurier and Scott-Moncrieff are compounds, but not Conan Doyle, Lloyd George, or Rider Haggard.

Occasionally, the student is misled by a hyphenated name that really combines the surnames of two people. For example, the collaborators, Emile Erckmann and Alexandre Chatrian are often put on title-pages as Erckmann-Chatrian. The absence of a forename should make the cataloguer investigate further.

In French hyphenated names the first part is sometimes a christian name and must be treated as such. Thus, Robert Jean-Boulan is entered as BOULAN, Robert Jean. No reference need be made from Jean-Boulan.

5. CHANGE OF SURNAME

Rules 40 and 41 are concerned with changed surnames, but No. 41, which deals with married women, is used far more frequently. Both give alternative rulings because the two Associations could not agree. In each rule; the British decision is to make entry under the earliest name used as an author, with reference or references from any later names.

When cataloguing books written by a married woman, the heading is apt to be rather long. For the actual entry under maiden name, the italicized (or underlined) words, *afterwards Mrs.*, and the married name are all given (*see* Examples 25 and 26, page 56).

Mary Elizabeth Braddon did publish under her maiden name, but Elizabeth Cleghorn Stevenson only published after marriage and only under her married surname. The rule says, "Enter a married woman under the earliest name she has used as an author. Refer from later names." Following this, we enter under Gaskell and omit all reference from Stevenson. According to directions for entry under a married woman's name, "The heading is to consist of (*a*) husband's surname, (*b*) own forenames, and (*c*) her maiden name, when known, in parenthesis."

e.g. GASKELL, *Mrs.* Elizabeth Cleghorn (Stevenson).

"When a woman uses her husband's forenames or initials in place of her own on the title-pages of her books, add this form in the heading and refer from it." The title *Mrs.* is not put before the authoress's forenames, as it appears later in the heading.

e.g. CHESTERTON, Ada Elizabeth (Jones) "*Mrs.* Cecil Chesterton".

e.g. HAWEIS, Mary Eliza (Joy) "*Mrs.* H. R. Haweis".

There will be references from CHESTERTON, *Mrs.* Cecil, and from HAWEIS, *Mrs.* H. R.

6. TITLES OF RANK

Change of name in a woman writer can be even more trying to cataloguers when she marries someone with a title. For instance, Mary Anne Stewart married and became Lady Barker. She published a book, *Travelling about over new and old ground* under that name. Her husband died and at last she remarried, thereby losing her title and becoming plain Mrs. Broome. Another complicated case is quoted by J. D. Brown, "Cecilia Francisca Josefa Bohl von Faber wrote several works under the name of Faber. Then she became Madame Planell, next the Marquesa de Arco-Hermoso, and afterwards Madame Arrom de Ayàlä." Strict interpretation of the A.A. rules results in catalogue entry under the following long heading:—

> FABER, Cecilia Francisca Josefa Bohl von, *afterwards* Mme Planell, *afterwards* marquesa de Arco-Hermoso, *afterwards* Mme Arrom de Ayàlä.

The 1941 revised code omits the married name or names from the heading (*see* 59 c), so entry according to that rule would be merely:—

FABER, Cecilia Francisca Josefa Bohl von.

In either case there would be *see* references from:—

(1) VON FABER, Cecilia Francisca Josefa Bohl.
(2) PLANELL, *Mme* Cecilia Francisca Josefa Bohl.
(3) ARCO-HERMOSO, Cecilia Francisca Josefa Bohl, *marquesa* de.
(4) HERMOSO, Cecilia Francisca Josefa Bohl, *marquesa* de Arco-.
(5) ARROM DE AYÀLÄ, *Mme* Cecilia Francisca Josefa Bohl.
(6) DE AYÀLÄ, *Mme* Cecilia Francisca Josefa Bohl Arrom.
(7) AYÀLÄ, *Mme* Cecilia Francisca Josefa Bohl Arrom de.

The A.A. rules for entry of titled authors are as follows:—

33 (British alternative) Enter a nobleman under his family name and refer from his titles.

34 Enter ecclesiastical dignitaries, except those mentioned in 31, under their surnames. In the case of bishops and archbishops of the Church of England, refer from the name of their sees.

35 Add in the heading titles and designations which indicate nobility and the higher offices or ranks when they are commonly used in referring to a person. Foreign titles are to be given in English when the forename is entry word, otherwise in the vernacular.

36 Add to the forename when it is used as entry word any epithet, by-name, or adjective of origin, nationality, etc., by which the person is usually known.

According to these rules sovereigns, and other persons of high rank who may be catalogued under the forename, are given the English form of their titles. Such titles follow the forename, also any reference to places connected with them.

A commonly used descriptive epithet may also be added, but this will precede the title, *e.g.* FRIEDRICH II, der Grosse, *king of Prussia*, and EDWARD VII, *king of Great Britain*.

Titles that follow the name are given in small letters, but most of those that come before it (*e.g. Mrs.*) are capitalized. Here the student will find it useful to turn to the Library of Congress supplementary rules, which follow Rule 172. Three of these deal with the capitalization of epithets and titles.

(*j*) Capitalize by-names affixed to and epithets standing in place of names of persons (*e.g.* Alexander the Great).

(*k*) In English and Dutch, capitalize titles of honour and distinction immediately preceding or standing instead of a person's name. They are not to be capitalized when placed after the name. In French, German, Italian, Spanish, and the Scandinavian languages such titles are to begin with a small letter whether they precede or follow the name. [*e.g.* Earl Spencer; Bishop of Albany; *but* James Stanley, 7th earl of Derby; Edward White Benson, archbishop of Canterbury; Otto fürst von Bismarck.] Abbreviations of titles of honour or distinction preceding personal names are to be capitalized in English, French, Dutch, and Spanish only.

(*l*) Capitalize titles of address, whether written in full or abbreviated, except in German and the Scandinavian languages.

All titles, epithets, etc., are to be printed in italics. In a written or typed catalogue, they should be underlined. This is to distinguish them from the name proper, and also to assist the person who files the entry.

Entry for ecclesiastical dignitaries is quite simple. If not entered under the forename, they come under Rule 34.

e.g. DIGGLE, J W , *bp. of Carlisle*.

A reference must be made from

  CARLISLE, J W Diggle, *bp. of*

The highest members of the English nobility are the dukes. Then come marquesses, earls, viscounts, barons, baronets, and knights. Only in the last two does a title precede the forename, *e.g. Sir* John Adye, and *Sir* John Dugdale, *bart*. Except for knights and baronets, and in cases where the holder of a title has been the only baron or viscount, etc., then the number must be included.

e.g. CAMPBELL, John Douglas Sutherland, 9*th duke of Argyll*.
VANE-TEMPEST-STEWART, Charles Stewart Henry, 7*th marquess of Londonderry*.
PLUNKETT, Edward John Moreton Drax, 19*th baron Dunsany*.

Cataloguing mistakes are often caused in the transcription of titled names. The student's attention is especially drawn to certain points that should be remembered. When the family name and the title are the same, both must be given. To make an entry, MACAULAY, Thomas Babington, *baron*, may lead to confusion, as Babington might easily be taken as the family name. The heading should be MACAULAY, Thomas Babington, *baron Macaulay*. Secondly, the full name and title must be given, even if this is abbreviated on a title-page. In transcribing the title, naturally the title-page version would be given, *e.g. Coningsby, by the Earl of Beaconsfield*. But the heading would be DISRAELI, Benjamin, 1*st earl of Beaconsfield*. Thirdly, the title *Lord* must not be used in headings for members of the British peerage. *Success, by Lord Beaverbrook*, is entered under AITKEN, William Maxwell, 1*st baron Beaverbrook*.

Quite different is the courtesy title of *Lord*, which is given from birth to younger sons of dukes and marquesses. This is easy to distinguish from the *Lord* used by peers, since it invariably precedes the forename, *e.g.* Lord Randolph Churchill, not Lord Churchill. Its use is perfectly correct in a heading, so, too, is the title *Honourable* (abbreviated to *Hon.*) for younger sons of earls.

e g. CHURCHILL, *Lord* Randolph Spencer.
(son of the Duke of Marlborough).
FINCH-HATTON, *Hon.* Harold
(son of the Earl of Winchilsea).

Daughters of dukes, marquesses and earls have the courtesy title *Lady*, and those of viscounts, *Hon.* The same rules apply.

e.g. EDGCUMBE, *Lady* Ernestine.

A woman who has this courtesy title retains it when she marries unless her husband has a higher rank. If a commoner marries a knight or baronet, she acquires the title *Lady*, but it is never placed before her forenames. She would be Lucie, Lady Duff-Gordon, for example, not Lady Lucie. In a catalogue entry, this title follows the forenames.

e.g. JEPHSON, Harriet Julia (Campbell), *lady*.

The wife of a duke, marquess, etc., takes the corresponding title to her husband, only there is no "number." He may be the ninth duke, but she will merely be described as duchess.

e.g. GRENVILLE, Alice Anne (Montgomery), *duchess of Buckingham and Chandos*.

Foreign titles are to be given in the vernacular when entry is made under the surname. *Deductions from the World war, by Lieutenant-General Baron von Freytag-Loringhoven*, has the catalogue heading

FREYTAG-LORINGHOVEN, Hugo, *freiherr von*.

The German title *Freiherr* is the equivalent of our *Baron*; *Graf* for *Earl* (or *Comte* in French); *Herzog* for *Duke*. *Prinz* and *Fürst* are even higher titles, but do not necessarily denote royal rank. For example, Prince Otto von Bismarck (more correctly Fürst Otto von Bismarck) is not a prince of the blood. A book by him would be catalogued under Rule 33, not Rule 32.

In all cases, references must be made from the titles (*see* Examples 27 and 28, page 57). The reference from the second half of the compound name can be omitted, since it is the same as this.

Below is an example of the entry of a titled woman author. This one did not write before marriage, so there is no need to make reference from her maiden name. In fact it is better to omit it altogether, as the heading is a long one (*see* Examples 29 and 30, page 58; Example 31, page 59).

7. VARIATIONS AND ASSUMED NAMES

Many writers try to conceal their identity by publishing their work anonymously (without author's name), or by using a false name, *i.e.* a pseudonym. The cataloguing of anonymous books, and a fuller treatment of pseudonymous, is dealt with in Chapter IV. Pseudonymous works are covered by A.A. Rule 38. Entry is only to be made under the pseudonym if the real name cannot be found, and there must be an added entry for the book's title. The 1941 revised Code has altered this rule so as to permit entry under the pseudonym when an author is far better known by the false than the real name, *e.g.* George Eliot. This modification is more in keeping with Rules 39, 43, and 44, where entry is permitted under a universally known sobriquet; under Greek and Latin forms adopted by writers of the Middle Ages, Renaissance, Reformation, and even in post-Reformation and modern times if the disguised name is better known. The same applies to a foreign form of name that the writer generally uses, or if an older transliterated form is better known (Rule 42).

8. GREEK, LATIN, AND ORIENTAL WRITERS

Rules 52–56 deal with Oriental writers. Here the general practice is to enter under the personal name, unless another form is better known in Western literature, or the author has adopted a surname in conformity with Western usage. These rules are inadequate for any library with a large Oriental collection, and they have been extended from one to eight pages in the 1941 revision. The beginner, however, need not concern himself with any further detail than is given in the original code.

The only remaining rules in this section are Nos. 49–51, which deal with classical and Byzantine writers. Ancient Greek are to be entered under the Latin form, and Byzantine under the Latin personal or baptismal name. The Latin form given in classical dictionaries is also the one to be used for classical Latin authors, *e.g.* VERGILIUS MARO, Publius; PLINIUS CAECILIUS SECUNDUS, Caius; OVIDIUS NASO, Publius. References must be made from popular forms, such as VERGIL, VIRGIL, PLINY, OVID.

EXAMPLES

23

		CLARENCE and Avondale, Albert Victor Christian Edward, prince, duke of. see ALBERT Victor Christian Edward, prince, duke of Clarence and Avondale.

See reference.

24

	KELLY, James Fitzmaurice-. <u>see</u>
FITZ	MAURICE-KELLY, James.

See reference.

25

	BRAD DON, Mary Elizabeth, afterwards Mrs. John Maxwell.
M.E.	The green curtain, by Braddon. London, Hutchinson and Co., 1911. iv,467p. 18½cm.

Married woman author—entry.

26

	MAXWELL, Mrs. John. <u>see</u>
	BRAD DON, Mary Elizabeth, afterwards Mrs. John Maxwell.

Married woman author—reference.

27

	BULWER-LYTTON, Edward George Earle Lytton, 1st baron Lytton.
	The last of the barons, by the Right Hon. Lord Lytton. London, George Routledge and Sons, [1843]. 633p. front. 19cm.

Titled author—main entry.

28

	LYTTON, Edward George Earle Lytton Bulwer-Lytton, 1st baron
	see
	BULWER-LYTTON, Edward George Earle Lytton, 1st baron Lytton.

Titled author—reference.

29

	GORDON, Ishbel Maria, mar-chioness of Aberdeen and Temair.
	Through Canada with a kodak. By the Countess of Aberdeen... Edinburgh, W.H. White and Co.,1893. 249p. front.,illus., photos,ports. 18½cm.

Titled woman author—main entry.

30

	ABERDEEN, Ishbel Maria Gordon, countess of see GORDON, Ishbel Maria, mar-chioness of Aberdeen and Temair.

Titled woman author—reference.

31

		ABERDEEN, Ishbel Maria
		Gordon, marchioness of
		see
	GORD	ON, Ishbel Maria, mar-
	chio	ness of Aberdeen and
	Tema	ir.

Titled woman author—reference.

CHAPTER IV

MAIN TITLE ENTRIES

1. DIFFERENCE BETWEEN ANONYMOUS AND PSEUDONYMOUS WORKS

THE A.A. definition of an anonymous work is one where "the author's name does not appear in the book itself," and of pseudonym "an assumed name under which a person writes." Rule 38 gives instructions for dealing with pseudonymous and Rules 112–118 with anonymous books, thus separating the two. Even so, it is difficult to decide which should be put in the former class and which excluded. Consider the following examples:—

(1) The Alternative / a Study in Psychology.
(2) The / Exiles at St. Germains. / By / The Author of / "The Ladye Shakerley."
(3) More Than Kin / A Novel / By M. P.
(4) Through North Wales / With A Knapsack / By / Four Schoolmistresses.
(5) To Justify the Means / By / A Peer.
(6) Two Bad Blue Eyes / A Novel / By / "Rita".

Title-page No. (1) has no author's name, nor any substitute for one. It is therefore anonymous in the strict meaning of the term, which excludes even pseudonymous works. No. (6) is pseudonymous, since "Rita" is obviously an assumed name. But in which group are Nos. (2) to (5) to be placed? Are *Author of "The Ladye Shakerley," M.P., Four Schoolmistresses,* and *A Peer* to be considered pseudonyms or not? The distinction is important because the A.A. code prescribes entry for pseudonymous works under the pseudonym but entry for anonymous under the first word of the title, which is not an article. These rulings only apply when the author's identity cannot be traced. If it is discovered, then, in both cases, entry must be made under the real name.

The 1941 revised code has a long *specification* at the beginning of the section on Anonymous works. This is worth quoting, since it clears up several difficulties.

"A strictly anonymous work is one in which the author's name does not appear anywhere in the book. The term is here extended to include (1) works in which the author's name does not appear on the title-page, but may occur, openly or concealed, elsewhere in the book; (2) works whose authorship is indicated by a descriptive or generic word or phrase preceded by an article, *e.g.* 'by a lover of justice,' 'by a physician,' 'by the lady from Philadelphia,' 'by a bishop of the Church of England'; (3) works in which instead of his name, the author gives the title of another of his books, *e.g.* 'by the author of . . .'; (4) those in which the author uses initials, asterisks, or other symbols instead of his name.

"Works in which an author uses *as a name* a specific word or phrase with or without a definite article are treated as pseudonymous."

A note to (2) explains that "The author's use of a title instead of his name, *e.g.* 'by the bishop of York,' 'by the secretary of state' does not constitute anonymity unless there is no evidence as to identity."

In a note to the revised Rule 38, which becomes No. 56 in the 1941 code, it is explained that a pseudonymous author "is one who writes under a false name" and that "The term is here extended to include those who conceal their identities" in the following ways:—

"(1) By assuming the name of another real person (allonym), *e.g.* 'by Horacio Flaco'; (2) by rearranging the letters of the name (anagram), *e.g.* 'by Olphar Hamst,' *i.e.* Ralph Thomas; or by adopting an inverted spelling . . .; by using forenames or forenames only, *e.g.* . . . 'by Anthony Berkeley,' *i.e.* Anthony Berkeley Cox; (4) by rearranging the order of surname and Christian names, *e.g.* 'by Leilani Jones Melville,' *i.e.* Melville Leilani Jones; (5) by using as a name a specific word or phrase with or without a definite article, *e.g.* 'by Acutus,' . . . 'by Operator 1384,' 'by the Duchess,' 'by the Prig,' etc."

It is very difficult for the cataloguer to make a distinction between this No. (5) and the No. (2) given in the specification of anonymous books. If the phrase or word is preceded by an indefinite article, like *a lover of justice*, or *a physician*, or *a peer*, it falls within the anonymous group. If there is no article, like *Ex-intelligence officer*, or *Cheiro*, it is pseudonymous. Where the phrase has a definite article at the beginning, the difference between anonymous and pseudonymous is still vague. According to examples given, *the lady from Philadelphia* is not a pseudonym, but *the Duchess* and *the Prig* are. The distinction—a very fine one—seems to lie in the word, or words, forming a distinguishing appellation. The last two appear to specify distinct individuals, but the longer phrase, although given a definite article, is not sufficiently distinctive. This is the only conclusion one can arrive at, and it is a pity the new code is not more explicit.

Cutter divides the two groups as follows: "A pseudonym is a false name; a phrase—'One who loves his country,' 'A friend to peace'—or even a shorter appellation—'A lawyer' is not a name. References might be made from these to the word under which the book is entered, but they would swell the catalog and rarely be of use. Appellatives beginning with the definite article, like 'The Prig,' 'The Old Shekarry,' 'The Duchess' are not vague like 'A lover of justice' and when constantly used should be treated as names in the way either of entry or reference."

Thus, in the examples quoted at the beginning of this chapter, *a peer* and *four schoolmistresses* are not to be regarded as false names, therefore (2) to (5) are catalogued according to the rules for anonymous works.

2. DISCOVERY OF AUTHORSHIP

If the real author of an anonymous or pseudonymous work can be discovered, then entry is made under the real name, which is enclosed in square brackets in the heading. There should also be added entry under the title of the work, and, if pseudonymous, a reference from the pseudonym. In the case of anonymous books, no reference is required from such "non-pseudonyms" as *a peer, a lover of justice,* etc. There are special rules for initials and the phrase *author of (see* Examples 32 to 36, pages 70 and 71).

In both cases, the title is transcribed exactly. No name is given in (*a*) since none appears on the title-page. In (*b*) the assumed name is given and to show why this differs from the heading, the word *pseud.* is added, italicized, and placed in square brackets.

Rule 38 of the original code should be strictly followed, unless the student is actually working in a library that uses the 1941 modifications and he has some knowledge of writers who can safely be entered under the pseudonym. A detailed search must be made for the real name, whether for entry or reference heading. A writer may publish one work anonymously, or under a pseudonym, then later others under his proper name. Unless the works of one author are collected under one heading, the author catalogue fails to answer the important question, "What works have you by So-and-so?"

3. UNDISCOVERED AUTHORSHIP

No. 38 of the A.A. code says, "Enter under the pseudonym of a writer when the real name is not known, and add the abbreviation *pseud.* in the heading. Make added entry under the title." No. 112 is the general rule for anonymous books and orders main entry under the first word of the title (other than an article), provided the author's name cannot be found. There is also provision for added entry under a particular person or place if the work specially relates to one, but, as the note explains, this is usually covered by a subject entry. The student can therefore omit this (*see* Examples 37 to 39, pages 72 and 73).

It will be noticed that the word *pseud.* is not included in the title as in the example for discovered authorship. This is not necessary here, as the pseudonym itself has been used as heading and the indication that it is a false name is given there.

4. SPECIAL CASES OF ANONYMOUS BOOKS

Rules 113–118 deal with special cases, such as reference to an earlier anonymous work, initials, different spelling for the first word of the title, related works, and translations. The last-named needs explanation. The two committees differed, the British rule being that entry for translations of an anonymous work should be under the same heading as that used for the original, *i.e.* in the original language presumably. This does not apply to national epics, etc., which come under Rule 120 and generally have the English form. They are dealt with in Section 5 of this chapter.

The most important of these rules are Nos. 114 and 115. No. 114 states: "When an anonymous work of undiscovered authorship bears on its title-page such a phrase as 'by the author of,' enter it under its title with an added entry under the title quoted, followed by the words 'Author of.' If different titles are thus used by an author at various times, make the added entry under the title most frequently referred to, or, in case of doubt, under one of his best known or earlier works. Refer from the title of each work to the title thus chosen, using the form: For other works by this author see . . ."

Thus, *A life's remorse . . . by the author of "Molly Bawn," "Phyllis," "The Honbl. Mrs. Vereker," Etc., Etc.*—provided the author's name cannot be found—has entry under LIFE'S with the reference note at the bottom of the card (*see* Examples 40 and 41, pages 73 and 74).

When authorship has been discovered, then entry is made under his, or her, name. For example, *Cameos from English history. The wars in France. By the author of "The heir of Redclyffe,"* has main entry under [YONGE, Charlotte Mary]. Added entry should be made under CAMEOS, but there is no need for one under HEIR *of Redclyffe, Author of*. If the library has a copy of *The heir*, then it would be entered under YONGE. If it, too, had been published anonymously, it would automatically have an added entry under title. Actually, it appeared under the author's own name.

Rule No. 115 covers initials, asterisks, and other typographical devices, which may be used in place of the author's name. Sometimes these stand for an actual name, often they have nothing to do with it. If undiscovered, entry is under title, with added entry (or reference) under first and last letters of the initials. Thus, *Guy Falconer; or, The chronicles of the old moat house. A battle of fortune. By L.E.G.* has main entry under GUY, and added entries under L.E.G. and under G., L.E.

The author of *Sylvana's letters to an unknown friend, by E.V.B.* is found to be the Hon. Mrs. Eleanor Vere Boyle, *née* Gordon. As this lady did not publish under her maiden name and E.V.B. obviously stands for Eleanor Vere Boyle, the main entry will be under BOYLE, *Hon. Mrs.* Eleanor Vere (Gordon). There will be added entries under SYLVANA'S; B., V.E.; and E.V.B. As authorship has been discovered, advantage could be taken of the alternative given in this rule and, instead of added entries, references could be made from B., V.E. and from E.V.B.

5. SACRED BOOKS AND ANONYMOUS CLASSICS

Sacred books, like the Bible or Koran, cause cataloguing difficulties because of their publication in different languages, in sections, and with notes and commentaries by numerous editors. As in works by one author, the principle applied is to collect everything under a single constant heading. Thus, Rule 119 says that the Bible or any part of it in any language is to be entered under the word BIBLE. Similarly, Old and New Testament are made divisions of this heading, and individual texts are subdivisions. *The Gospel according to St. Matthew, edited by the Rev. A. Carr,* has its main entry heading, BIBLE. *New Testament. Gospel according to St. Matthew,* while there is an added entry under CARR, A , ed. Language makes no difference, except that the name of the language is added as a further subdivision. *Testament Newydd* is entered as BIBLE. *New Testament. Welsh.* A scheme of arrangement is given and here the subheadings are all put in italics. The cataloguer is also told to "refer from titles of individual parts or books, especially when they have been published separately."

e.g.   NEW TESTAMENT
        see
    BIBLE. *New Testament.*

e.g.   GOSPEL ACCORDING TO ST. MATTHEW
        see
    BIBLE. *New Testament. Gospel according to St. Matthew.*

e.g.   MATTHEW, *Saint, Gospel according to,*
        see
    BIBLE. *New Testament. Gospel according to St. Matthew.*

Besides the "sacred books," there are several groups of epics and folk tales, which have well-known, traditional names, *e.g.* the *Nibelungenlied, Reynard the fox.* These have been translated into numerous languages and are often better known in this country under a translated title, *e.g. Arabian nights,* rather than *Alif laila.* The revised code calls these *anonymous classics* and defines such a work as one "of unknown or doubtful authorship, commonly designated by title, which may have appeared in the course of time in many editions, versions, and/or translations." The following entries from the Edinburgh University Library catalogue will show the necessity of collecting whole and part copies of such a work under one heading.

ARABIAN NIGHTS
  Tausend und eine Nacht. Arabisch . . . Hrsg. von M. Habicht. (Nach seinem Tode fortgesetzt von H. L. Fleischer.) 12 Bde.
    8° Breslau, 1825-43.
  The Alif Laila; or, Book of the thousand nights and one night, commonly known as "The Arabian Nights' entertainments"; now . . . published . . . in the original Arabic, from an Egyptian manuscript brought to India by . . . Major Turner Macan . . . Ed. by W. H. Macnaghten. 4 vols.
    W. P. Grant, 1845. 8° Calcutta, 1839-42.
  Histoire d' 'Alâ Al-Dîn, ou, la lampe merveilleuse. Texte arabe, publié avec une notice sur quelques manuscrits des Mille et une nuits, par H. Zotenberg. *Facs.*
    8° Paris, 1888.
  [The Arabian Nights' entertainments. Tr. . . . by Dinendra Kumar Ray.] *Bengali.* 3 vols.
    8° [Calcutta, 1899.]
  A plain and literal translation of the Arabian Nights' entertainments, now entituled: The book of the thousand nights and a night. With introd., notes . . . and . . . essay upon the history of the Nights . . . by R. F. Burton. (Ill. Benares ed., *etc.,* issued by the Burton Club.) 10 vols.
    8° pr. by the Burton Club, n.d.
  Supplemental Nights . . . With notes . . . by R. F. Burton. (Ill. Benares ed., *etc.*) 7 vols.
    8° pr. by the Burton Club, n.d.
  The Arabian Nights' entertainments . . . Freely transcribed

[by C. D. Piguenit] from the original translation. Vols. 1-2 (in 1).
   8° Lond., 1792.
   Pp. 249-251 of vol. 2 mutilated; vols. 3-4 wanting.
The thousand and one nights . . . A new tr. from the Arabic, with . . . notes, by E. W. Lane. Ill. by . . . engravings . . . from original designs by W. Harvey. 3 vols.
   8° Lond., 1841, 40-41.

Rule 120 advises entry of anonymous classics under the English name, with reference from the vernacular. If the vernacular is better known, choose that and refer from the English form. In either case there will be added entries under editors, translators, etc. Following the A.A. code, the fifth example quoted from the Edinburgh University Library catalogue would have entries and references (*see* Examples 42 to 44, pages 74 and 75).

6. PERIODICALS AND OTHER SERIAL PUBLICATIONS

The definition of a periodical in the 1941 revision is clearer and better worded than that in the original code. "A publication with a distinctive title intended to appear in successive (usually unbound) numbers or parts at stated or regular intervals and, as a rule, for an indefinite time. Each part generally contains articles by several contributors. *Newspapers*, whose chief function is to disseminate news, and the *Memoirs*, *Proceedings*, *Journals*, etc., of societies are not considered periodicals under the rule."

According to Rule 121, the main entry for a periodical is under the first word of its title, not an article. Added entries are to be made for editors and compilers of indexes. Directions are also given for certain notes on frequency of publication, etc., and analytical entries for monograph supplements. These will be dealt with in Chapter VI. The two committees differed over the treatment of periodicals that change their name, and

MAIN TITLE ENTRIES 69

the British rule is to enter under the earlier form with brief entries under later forms. If a periodical issued by a society or an institution has a distinctive title, then that is entered like an independent periodical, under the title. Collections of extracts from a periodical follow the same heading, with added entries under title of the collection and name of the collector. But the rule (No. 122) stipulates that if the periodical is not named in the title, main entry is to be made under the name of the collector, or title if anonymous.

Libraries usually wait until the separate parts of a periodical have been bound into a volume before making a catalogue entry (*see* Example 45, page 75).

If the set had been complete and the library still taking it, the entry would have been given as Vol. 1 and the words *to date* added.

The term *serial* is of wider extension and includes periodicals annuals, year-books, newspapers, etc. Its definition is "a publication issued in successive parts, usually at regular intervals, and, as a rule, intended to be continued indefinitely." Nearly all serial publications, including publishers' series (set of volumes issued in uniform style with a collective title and usually related in subject-matter), have main entry under title. (*See* Rules 123, 124, 125, and 128.) An exception is made for a non-periodical directory that has its compiler's name mentioned on the title-page.

A publication that is continued indefinitely may have several changes of editorship over a long period of time. Title entry is stable and the work likely to be better known by his title. For example, *The writers' and / artists' year book / 1929 / a directory for writers / artists and photographers / edited by Agnes Herbert / twenty-second year of / new issue /* should be entered under WRITERS, with added entry under HERBERT, Agnes, *ed.*

7. COLLECTIONS, ENCYCLOPAEDIAS, INSCRIPTIONS

Nos. 126, 127, and 129 are the remaining rules in Section (*d*) of the A.A. code. Although this section is called *Title Entry*, main entry under editor or collector is preferred in these three cases. Exceptions are made where the work is better known by title, or if the editor's part is very slight.

EXAMPLES

32

```
[LUKIN, James.]
     The lathe and its uses;
or,  Instruction in the art of
turning wood and metal...
Fourth edition.    London,
Trubner and Co.,1874.
     315p.     front.,illus.
21½cm.
```

Anonymous author—main entry.

33

```
     LATHE.
[LUKIN, James.]
     The lathe and its uses;
or,  Instruction in the art of
turning wood and metal...
Fourth edition.    London,
Trubner and Co., 1874.
     315p.     front.,illus.
21½cm.
```

Anonymous author—added entry.

MAIN TITLE ENTRIES   71

34

[VIAUD, Louis M   J   ]
    Madame Chrysanthème, par
Pierre Loti [pseud.]...
Trente-deuxième édition.
Paris, Calmann Lèvy, 1895.
    [vi], [305]p.   19cm.

Pseudonymous author—main entry.

35

MADAME.
[VIAUD, Louis M   J   ]
    Madame Chrysanthème, par
Pierre Loti [pseud.] Trente-
deuxième édition.   Paris,
Calmann Lèvy, 1895.
    [vi], [305]p.   19cm.

Pseudonymous author—added entry.

36

LOTI, Pierre, pseud.
        see
[VIAUD, Louis M   J   ]

Pseudonymous author—reference.

37

	GREAT.
	The great secret: being letters of an old man to a young woman: a book for beginners... London, Watts and Co., 1911. xi,[i],247p. 20cm.
the
a yo
begi
Watt

Anonymous author—main entry when authorship cannot be found.
No added entries or references required.

38

	ELLANGOWAN, pseud.
	Out-door sports in Scotland: deer stalking, grouse shooting, salmon fishing, golfing, curling, etc..., by ''Ellangowan''. Second edition... London, W.H. Allen and Co., 1890. xi,388p. front.,plan. 19cm.
land
shoo
golf
by '
edit
Alle
19cm

Pseudonymous author—main entry.

MAIN TITLE ENTRIES 73

39

		OUT-DOOR.
	ELLANGOWAN, pseud.	
		Out-door sports in Scotland: deer stalking, grouse shooting, salmon fishing, golfing, curling, etc..., by ''Ellangowan''. Second edition... London, W.H. Allen and Co., 1890
		xi,388p. front.,plan. 19cm.

Pseudonymous author—added entry.

40

		LIFE'S.
		A life's remorse: a novel. By the author of ''Molly Bawn''... London, R.E. King, [189-?]
		320p. 17½cm.
		For other works by this author, see MOLLY BAWN, Author of.

Anonymous author—main entry.

41

		MOLLY Bawn, Author of.
	LIFE	'S
	By the	A life's remorse: a novel.
	Bawn	author of ''Molly
	R.E.	''... London,
		King, [189-?]
		320p. 17½cm.
		Also author of ''Phyl-
		lis'', ''The Honble. Mrs.
		Vereker'', etc., etc.

Anonymous author—added entry.

42

		ARABIAN NIGHTS.
	lati	A plain and literal trans-
	ente	on of the Arabian Nights'
	The	rtainments, now entituled:
	nigh	book of the thousand
	intr	ts and a night. With
	essa	oduction, notes...and...
	Nigh	y upon the history of the
	Bena	ts... by R.F.Burton.
		res, Burton Club, [n.d.]
		10v. 20?cm.

Anonymous classics—main entry.

MAIN TITLE ENTRIES 75

43

	ed.	BURTON, Sir Robert F , and tr.
	ARABIAN NIGHTS. A plain and literal translation of the Arabian nights' entertainments, now entituled: The book of the thousand nights and a night. With introduction, notes...and... essay upon the history of the Nights... by R. F. Burton. Benares, Burton Club, [n.d.] 10v. 20?cm.	

Anonymous classics—added entry.

44

		ALIF LAILA see
	ARABIAN NIGHTS.	

Anonymous classics—reference.

45

	CORNHILL.	
	Vols 1860	The Cornhill magazine. . 1-6, 18-46. London, -82. Number for July 1880 in Vol. 42 is wanting.

Periodicals—main entry.

CHAPTER V

CORPORATE AUTHORSHIP

1. DEFINITION OF CORPORATE ENTRY

THE A.A. code has two meanings of the word *author*. In the narrow sense, this is "the writer of the book, as distinguished from translator, editor, etc." The broader conception of the term covers, "the maker of the book or the person or body immediately responsible for its existence." An editor may be considered *author* of an anthology that he has compiled, *e.g.* Palgrave is the author of the *Golden treasury* . . . Similarly, a corporate body, such as a government or a society, who is directly responsible for the production of certain publications connected with its work, is usually regarded as the author for cataloguing purposes.

The A.A. code defines corporate entry as "entry under the names of bodies or organizations for works published in their name or by their authority."

2. KINDS OF CORPORATE AUTHORSHIP

Corporate authors are divided into four groups in the A.A. code, (*a*) Government bodies, (*b*) Societies, (*c*) Institutions, and (*d*) Miscellaneous corporate bodies.

Section (*a*) includes national and local governments, but excludes certain institutions, etc., that a government may maintain or control. For example, the Church of England is a state church, but in cataloguing it is treated like other religious organizations and entered with societies. Likewise, the British Museum is entered according to the rules of institutions in section (*c*).

Examples in the code show the use of the heading GREAT

BRITAIN, not ENGLAND, for British government publications. The student should note that these may be parliamentary or non-parliamentary. The former includes acts, command papers, and reports that are issued by, or with the sanction of both Houses of Parliament. The word *Parliament* is given as a sub-heading. Non-parliamentary publications are issued by the various departments of state, *e.g. Department of scientific and industrial research, Ministry of health*, or commissions, *e.g. Historical manuscripts commission.* Entry is best made without any inversion, *e.g.* GREAT BRITAIN. *Ministry of health*, not *Health, Ministry of*. All department sub-headings are printed in italics (*see* Example 46, pages 88 and 89).

Government bureaux and offices are often made subordinate to another department as a temporary convenience. There is no need for this to be carried out in the catalogue, hence Rule 59, which says they are to be entered directly under the country, *e.g.* GREAT BRITAIN. *Meteorological office*, not GREAT BRITAIN. *Air ministry. Meteorological office.* The general rule for government publications is No. 58, "Enter under names of countries, states, cities, towns, etc., official publications issued by them or under their auspices. The names of departments, bureaux, etc., from which the publications emanate are to be given as subheadings." A note after "towns, etc.," refers the reader to Rule 130, which orders geographical names to be given in the English form when used as entry words. If a vernacular form is used as well in English books, then this may be preferred.

Section (*b*) covers societies. Here, entry is made under the first part of the society's name, provided this is not an article,

e.g. SOCIETY FOR THE DIFFUSION OF USEFUL KNOWLEDGE, London.

e.g. ROYAL ASTRONOMICAL SOCIETY OF LONDON.

Reference should be made from the name of the place where the society is located. If not part of the name, this is added in the main heading in italics after a comma, if deemed necessary. Reference can also be made from any other name by which the society is known. School and college societies are entered under the institution concerned. But the one exception to name entry in independent societies is the rule for guilds (77). These are to be entered under the name of the city with the company's name as a sub-heading.

Institutions in section (c) fall into two main groups, those under place and those under name. Rule 82 says, "Enter an institution under the name of the place in which it is located," and Rule 83, "Enter an institution whose name begins with a proper noun or adjective under the first word of its name, and refer from the name of the place where it is located" (*see* Examples 47 to 49, pages 89 and 90).

Section (d), Miscellaneous corporate bodies, covers a variety of conferences, occasional meetings, expeditions, etc., that are not connected with any government, society, or institution. Such bodies are without a continued existence and the rule may order their entry under name or under place of meeting, as best suits the case.

The A.A. rules for corporate bodies extend from Nos. 58–111 in the original code; from Nos. 71–191 in the 1941 revision. A few important rules have been quoted here, but the cataloguer must study the code itself for the many varieties of corporate authorship.

3. DISTINGUISHING THE TYPES OF CORPORATE AUTHORSHIP

One of the difficulties facing the cataloguer in dealing with corporate authorship is to decide the group of a work, according to the A.A. sectional divisions. Is its issuing body a government, or a society, or an institution? In the first case, it will be entered under the region governed, in the second under its name, and in the third entry will be under place of location or again under name.

The student should first note the exception to country, state, or town entry for "certain classes of institutions and other bodies created, maintained, controlled or owned by governments." These exceptions are only mentioned in the 1941 revision, "*e.g.* colleges, universities, schools, libraries, museums, galleries, observatories . . ., churches, societies, etc." They are to be treated according to the rules for societies or institutions, as the case may be.

The 1941 revision of the A.A. code defines a society as "an organization of persons associated together for the promotion of common purposes or objects, such as research, business, recreation, etc." Institutions (or establishments) are "entities whose functions require a plant with buildings, apparatus, etc., as distinguished from bodies, organized groups of persons such as societies, associations, etc., whose duties may be performed equally well in one place or another. The necessity of having a permanent material equipment tends to identify the institution with a locality."

These distinctions are not completely satisfactory because some corporate bodies fit into both classes. For example, a university is strictly speaking a society. Universities were formed by bands of learned men who joined together for purposes of study. Later they became teachers as well as research workers, and each university now has become associated with a particular place. There its work is carried on in buildings set aside for that purpose. Thus, universities are classed as institutions in the A.A. code, along with colleges, schools, libraries, museums, art galleries, monasteries, etc. Normally these are entered under place of location, unless the institution's name begins with a proper noun or adjective. In the 1941 revision, these exceptions are limited to institutions of the United States and British Empire only. Even so, they are sufficiently numerous to confuse readers who never know whether to look under name or place in the catalogue.

Under the term societies are included associations, academies, and usually institutes; an institute originally meant a society. Thus, the Royal institute of international affairs is a society, so are the American academy of arts and sciences at Boston, and the Royal college of surgeons, London. These are entered under the name, with reference from place (Rule 72). The Smithsonian institution, Washington, is an institution and should be entered under place (Rule 82), but, as its name begins with a proper noun, it is entered under that name (Rule 83).

4. CHANGE OF NAME

Change of name may occur in a country, so when confronted with government publications the cataloguer is in a difficulty. Shall all the material already catalogued under PERSIA or RUSSIA be transferred to the new heading IRAN or U.S.S.R.? The usual practice is to retain the old heading for material published prior to the change, and to add a *see also* reference after the entries. A *see also* card will also be inserted after entries under the new heading,

e.g.   RUSSIA
                see also
         U.S.S.R.

As explained in Chapter III, section 1, the *see also* reference is used to show where other connected material may be found.

The use of the *see also* here may seem contrary to the practice of keeping together all the work of an individual author who changes his name. There, entry is made under the earliest name used for authorship, with *see* references from later names, instead of following the title-pages and merely linking the various entries by *see also* references. Normally, entry under one heading, with *see* references from those not used, is more satisfactory to the reader. He prefers to find the novels of Fanny Burney together, not to have to look for *Evelina* under Burney and *Camilla* under Arblay. Copies of the *Arabian nights* are better collected under that heading, not scattered under a variety of titles. But in the case of works by an individual, or different publications of an anonymous work, there is a unity that justifies this. Certain characteristics remain in the writings of a person, even if he or she changes his or her name. A French copy of the *Arabian nights* does not become an entirely different work through being translated into another language.

When countries change their names the publications of their governments may be completely altered in scope and character. A society or an institution becoming absorbed by a government body may do quite different work, and its books and pamphlets issued under the old name have no interest for those studying its new projects. The presence of many cards moved from old heading to new may be a source of confusion to readers consulting the catalogue. The student must remember that publications by a corporate body are usually far more numerous than those under an individual, since the country, or society, or institution, has a far longer life.

Change of name in a corporate author may be much more extensive in its effects. Two societies may join together. For example, the Philosophical society of Victoria amalgamated with the Victorian institute of science. Shortly afterwards, the name they adopted, the Philosophical institute of Victoria, was changed to Royal society of Victoria. In 1887, this absorbed the Microscopical society of Victoria. Instead of changing the entries for all publications of these different societies before 1887, entry under each, with *see also* references to and from Royal society of Victoria, is the best way out of the confusion.

The A.A. code has a rule (89b) for collections that pass from the possession of a private person to a society or institution. Then "entry for all subsequent publications is to be made under the name of that body, with references from the name of the collection and the original collector. Publications issued before the change of ownership are to have added entry under the name of the institution or other body into whose possession the collection has passed." This is a common-sense rule because, as time goes on, the collection becomes completely identified with the corporate body who possesses it, and the individual tends to be forgotten.

For example, the basis of the Royal Dublin society's museum was the mineralogy collection of a man called Leske. Catalogue main entry heading would therefore be Royal Dublin Society. *Museum. Leske collection.* If Leske himself had issued a catalogue of the collection, then this would be entered under the same heading with the name of Leske above, making the entry into an added one. But if no catalogue had been issued before the Royal Dublin society gained possession, then there would only be a *see* reference from Leske, and one from Dublin. This, however, is not the end The museum was transferred to the Department of agriculture and technical instruction for Ireland, and at that date Ireland was under the government of Great Britain. With the establishment of the Irish Free State, this department became Department of education. Later publications would be under the headings, GREAT BRITAIN. *Department of agriculture* . . . and IRISH FREE STATE (or EIRE, if that was preferred) and sub-heading, *Department of education*, and there would be connecting *see also* references.

5. CORPORATE OR INDIVIDUAL ENTRY

Rule 60 of the A.A. code says that reports made to a government department by someone who is not an official should have main entry under the individual writer and only added entry under the department. A note extends this further:—

"This rule may be applied also in dealing with publications of private firms or companies, the main entry usually being made under the name of the firm when the compiler or editor is a regular official and the work of compilation or editing is a part of his official duties. On the other hand, main entry is made under the individual when it is known that the work is his own private publication. In either cases, added entry or reference is made under the party not selected as main heading."

All corporate publications are affected by this alternative and the cataloguer is forced to spend time in discovering the status of the individual, or individuals, named on the title-page before he can decide on this problem of authorship. For example, a title-page reads, *Department of Scientific and Industrial Research / Geological Survey and Museum / British Regional Geology: The Wealden District / By / F. H. Edmunds, M.A.* Is F. H. Edmunds an official or not? If he is, has this work been part of his official duties?

S. R. Ranganathan, in *Theory of library catalogue*, speaks of this difficulty.

"A treatise by a full-time salaried professor of a university is of Personal Authorship, although he produces it in his official time and as his sole official duty and the university publishes it at its own cost. But a report on the work of the Professor by a Review Committee appointed by the University is of Corporate Authorship. Even a report by the professor on the work of a research fellow of the university is of Corporate Authorship. Again, the annual report of the Director of an Archaeological Survey is of Corporate Authorship but a memoir by him on a particular find is of personal authorship though he produced both in his official time and as a salaried officer.

"May we say that a work whose primary function is extension of the sphere of knowledge should be taken to be of Personal Authorship while a work limited by its administrative purpose, function and outlook is of Corporate Authorship? This certainly provides a sharper test. But cases may still arise which will evade it. For example in a speech delivered by a Prime Minister before a learned body the official administrative element and the element of personal research may be inextricably interfused. The annual presidential addresses of many learned societies are in fact of this baffling type."

If the book is going to be well known, and readers are likely to ask for it, under the individual name, then there is certainly a strong case for putting the main entry under that name, e.g. *Ministry of Agriculture and Fisheries / Bulletin No. 126 / Report / on / Fungus, Bacterial and / Other Diseases of Crops / in England and Wales / for the Years /* 1933–1942 */ W. C. Moore, M.A. / (Ministry of Agriculture and Fisheries / Plant Pathology, Laboratory, Harpenden) / London / H.M.S.O. /* 1944. But, as Moore is obviously an official and the work is published by the government, main entry must be under GREAT BRITAIN: *Ministry of agriculture and fisheries*, with added entry under MOORE.

Here are some other examples:—

(1) The Assyrian Laws / Edited with / Translation and Commentary / by G. R. Driver and John C. Miles / Oxford / At the Clarendon Press / 1935.
(2) Hints to Travellers / Scientific and General / Edited for the / Council of the Royal Geographical Society / by / Douglas W. Freshfield, Hon. Sec. R.G.S., / and / Captain W. J. L. Wharton, R.N., F.R.S., / Hydrographer to the Admiralty / Sixth Edition / Revised and Enlarged / London, / The Royal Geographical Society . . .
(3) Land Settlement / a Report / prepared for the / Carnegie United Kingdom / Trustees / by / A. W. Menzies-Kitchin, M.A., B.Sc., / Farm Economics Branch, School of Agriculture / Cambridge University / With a foreword by the

Trustees / Edinburgh / Printed by T. and A. Constable Ltd. / 1935.

Example (1) contains the full text of the laws, so, according to Rule 13, it must be catalogued under the author of the text. Laws come under Rule 62 and are to be entered under the name of the country or state.

Main entry   ASSYRIA. *Laws.*
Added entry   DRIVER, G   R   , ed.
Added entry   MILES, John C   , ed.

Example (2) is produced by a society and one of its editors is the honorary secretary.

Main entry   ROYAL GEOGRAPHICAL SOCIETY, *London.*
Added entry   FRESHFIELD, Douglas W   , ed.
Added entry   WHARTON, W   J   L   , ed.
Reference (see) LONDON. Royal geographical society.

Example (3) appears to be a report by a non-official of the C.U.K.T. Main entry is therefore under the individual.

Main entry   MENZIES-KITCHIN, A   W
Added entry   CARNEGIE united kingdom trust.
Reference (see) KITCHIN, A   W   Menzies-.

The most difficult type of publication is one where a variety of bodies and individuals have taken part. The following is an extreme example. The only satisfactory heading seems Greenland, but this would be a subject entry and our main entry must be under author. *Bibliography / of Greenland / Section on / Medicine and Health / The Annotated Bibliography of the Polar Regions / Sponsored by / The United States Department of State / Co-sponsored by / The United States Department of War / Under the guidance of / The Bibliography Committee of / The Explorers Club / S. Whittemore Boggs / Herbert J. Spinden / Leonard Outhwaite / Vilhjalmur Stefansson / Prepared by W.P.A. Official Project Number / 165-2-97-69 W.P. 1 / James*

86   FUNDAMENTALS OF PRACTICAL CATALOGUING

Ferrell, Project Supervisor and Editor / New York, October 1942. The foreword is signed with the initials J. F. Cover-title reads, *Bibliography of Greenland / Medicine and Health / Federal Works Agency / Work Projects Administration / for the City of New York.*

6. THE PRACTICE OF GERMAN LIBRARIES

German libraries and most of those in surrounding countries, such as Austria, Switzerland and Holland, have always been opposed to the principle of corporate authorship. Where an individual's name appears on the title-page, he is regarded as the author, however slight his contribution to the book. If no individual is named, then the work is treated as anonymous and given title entry. This principle was established in the rules of Dziatzko (1886) and continued in the *Instruktionen für die alphabetischen Kataloge der preussischen Bibliotheken* (1908), commonly known in this country as the *Prussian instructions*. One of its basic rules excludes entry under a corporate body. "Names of persons, official bodies, corporations, etc., at whose instigation or with whose support the work has originated are disregarded."

e.g. Amgueddfa Genedlaethol Cymru / National Museum of Wales / Studies in the Origin of the Scenery of Wales. / 1—The River Scenery / at the Head of / the Vale of Neath / By F. J. North, D.Sc., F.G.S. / Second Edition / Cardiff, / Published by the National Museum of Wales and / by the Press Board of the University of Wales. / 1938.
    Extract from preface, "This is the fifth of a series of Museum publications, by the Keeper of the Department of Geology . . ."

F. J. North is therefore an official of the National museum of Wales, and, as the Museum has published the work, it is to be assumed that he undertook it as part of his official duties.

National institutions (Rule 90) are entered in the A.A. code under name of country, with place of location added after the institution's name. Catalogue entries according to this code would be as follows:—

Main entry WALES. National museum of Wales, *Cardiff*.
Added entry NORTH, F J
Reference (see) CARDIFF. National museum of Wales.

Catalogued by the Prussian instructions, the only entry would be under NORTH.

e.g. Report / on the / Imperial Entomological Conference / June 1920 / Presented to Parliament by Command of His Majesty / July 1920. / London, H.M.S.O. / 1920.

This conference of official entomologists in the Dominions, India, and the Colonies was convened by the Secretary of State for Colonies. A.A. code would have as main entry heading

> GREAT BRITAIN. *Colonial office. Imperial entomological conference*, 1920.

German libraries would treat this publication as anonymous and enter under title. Their rules for title entry are much more elaborate, main entry being made under the *Hauptsinnwort*. One cataloguer might choose *imperial*, another *entomological*, and a third *conference*, and the rest of the title would be inverted accordingly, *e.g.* Imperial entomological conference, June 1920, Report on.

Certainly, the German practice saves much time in deciding the type of corporate authorship into which the publication must be classed; whether it is a case of personal or corporate authorship, and so on. The A.A. rule for title entry—first word not an article—is very simple. Following that, the above example would be entered under REPORT. It is also argued that the number of cards under country headings will become so large as to be unmanageable, particularly as the functions of the state increase. Personal author and title headings are far easier for readers to understand and remember than the involved headings and sub-headings of corporate authors.

Against this, we have a long-established custom (since the days of Panizzi and Jewett) in Britain and the U.S.A. Moreover, it is convenient to have together the official publications of a state, or those sponsored by a society or institution. Cutter states the case for corporate authorship admirably in his *Rules for a dictionary catalog*, prior to Rule 45. He points out, too, the inconvenience of the German arrangement.

"If you want to find in Kayser's list of the books published in Germany in the last five years all the publications of a German learned body you must look under Abhandlungen, Almanach, Annalen, Arbeiten, Archiv . . . Vorlesungen, and Zeitschrift." Cutter lists forty of these words and then adds, "and if by racking your brain you remember all of them and have patience to look them all up, you yet are not sure that there is not something important hidden away under some other word which you may think of when it is too late—Verhandlungen, for instance."

EXAMPLES

46

The / Public General Acts / and the / Church Assembly Measures / of / 1942 / Being those which received the Royal Assent / in the / Fifth, Sixth and Seventh Years of the Reign of / His Majesty / King George the Sixth / In the Seventh and Part of the Eighth Session / of the Thirty-Seventh Parliament of the / United Kingdom of Great Britain and Northern Ireland / with / Tables of the Short Titles and of / The Effect of Legislation / and an Index /. H.M.S.O., / 1943.

46

GREAT BRITAIN. Parliament.
 Acts
 and
 measures
 tables
 and
 tion
 H.M.
. The public general acts and the Church assembly of 1942... with of the short titles of the effect of legislation and an index. [London], S.O., 1943.
 a-d,246,xxxiip.   25cm.

Government publications—main entry.
The abbreviation H.M.S.O. for *His Majesty's Stationery Office* may be retained.

47

ABERDEEN. University.
 Library
 rules
 University
 Second
 Aberdeen
 1924
. Condensed cataloguing as followed in the Library, Aberdeen. edition revised. , University Press,
 32p.   21½cm.

Rule 82—main entry.

48

	BRIT	ISH MUSEUM, London.
		... A guide to the Egyptian collections in the British museum. [London], Printed by order of the Trustees, 1909.
		xiv,325p. illus., plates,map. 21½cm.

Rule 83—main entry.

49

		LONDON. British museum.
		see BRITISH MUSEUM, London.

Rule 83—reference.

CHAPTER VI

CONTENTS. NOTES. ANALYTICS

1. CONTENTS

WHEN a single work occupies several volumes, it is a help to the reader if each volume's contents are stated on the main and added entry cards. He may not know which volume he requires and this saves him searching through the entire set. Often oversize books are kept on closed shelves, so to send for ten folios instead of one merely wastes the time of the assistant who fetches them. Again, several volumes of the set may be on loan to other readers and this inquirer have no idea which one he wants to reserve.

Contents should also be given for part collections of a single author, *e.g. Three plays for puritans, by Bernard Shaw*; for any work by several authors in which each makes a separate contribution, *e.g. Eight modern plays, selected and edited by John Hampden*; and even a single work on several subjects.

Rule 167 of the A.A. code includes clear directions and examples to show how contents should be set out. "Give contents in the order in which they appear in the book, and in paragraph form rather than in columns except in special cases where the latter arrangement has decided advantages. In case different parts are written by different authors, let the name of the author follow rather than precede the title, provided always this is the order of arrangement in the book."

The contents note is begun half a centimetre below the last line of the entry. The word *contents* starts at the inner margin, is put in italics (*i.e.* underlined in a written or typed catalogue) and is followed by a colon. Then come the details of content, these being taken back to the outer margin and each item separated by a long dash. Quite one centimetre upwards from the bottom of the card should be left blank, except for the words (Continued on next card), as the lower part is difficult to see when standing upright in a catalogue drawer. When continuing on a second card, number this (2), repeat heading and brief title, followed by a space of two centimetres and *Contents (continued)*. Leave the half a centimetre and then begin to list the remainder of contents without any paragraph indention to the inner margin.

Contents need not be given when these are stated as part of the title, *e.g. Confessions of an opium eater. (With "Levana" and "History of Rosicrucians and Freemasons") By Thomas De Quincey*. Nor are they usually necessary for collected works of an author when these are contained in a single volume.

2. NOTES

The object of catalogue notes is to give more information than can be provided in the entry. An entry consists of heading (for filing the card) and description of the book. This description is based on information taken from the title-page and certain physical features. The title-page must be followed exactly (although judicious omissions are allowed) and details of pagination, illustrations, and size are normally given as *collation*. Contents and notes are extras to the entry. Contents are limited to a statement in the order in which these items appear in the book. Notes are freer and more individual. Some catalogues use them frequently, others not at all. Their length varies as much as their purpose. Some catalogues only give notes of bibliographical interest, others only of a popular nature.

A.A. Rule 168 says they should be added "when necessary to explain the title or to correct any misapprehension to which it might lead, and also to supply essential information about the author and bibliographical details not given in the title, imprint, or collation." They must be in English, except for foreign quotations. Then comes a list of cases where notes are generally required, *e.g.* variations in title, imperfections in copy, etc. Furthermore, the 1941 revision urges brevity so far as clearness is not affected. With the exception of rare books and special bibliographies, notes should be limited to about thirty words. Lengthy notes in a card catalogue are difficult to read when they continue on several cards, while they add to the costs of printed lists. A cataloguer must acquire the habit of putting his information concisely. He is allowed, too, to omit unessential articles and adjectives. For example, "Some recollections of the author's happy childhood" can be cut down to "Recollections of author's childhood." Instead of "There is a one-page bibliography," simply write "Bibliography 1 p.," or "Bibliog. 1 p."

A note has the same position on the catalogue card as the statement of contents. It begins at the inner margin, with a space of half a centimetre between its top line and the last line of entry. Second and subsequent lines of note are taken out to the first margin. There are two exceptions to this practice. The series note is given as part of the entry and follows the collation in parenthesis. A space of two centimetres is left between them. This was explained in Chapter I, section 7. Notes of one or two words may be incorporated in the title part of the entry. They are then enclosed in square brackets to show they are not found on the title-page.

e.g. by Currer Bell [*pseud.*]
Uusi testamenti [Finnish.]
Royal flush: the story of Minette. By Margaret Irwin. [Historical novel.]

There are two kinds of note, the *bibliographical* and the so-called *literary*. The latter gives details of author and subject-matter to interest both student and leisured reader. Often the chief purpose is to attract the latter and "whet his appetite."

Such annotation is popular in the printed reading guides and book-lists that municipal and county libraries frequently issue. A limited number may also appear in individual card catalogues, while a few libraries use them extensively, even adding brief criticisms and extracts from reviews.

Bibliographical notes draw attention to unusual features of the book's make-up, details of publication, and facts about the text that may interest the student. Many of these are prescribed by A.A. code rules.

Missing title-pages, more than one title-page, change of title (*see* Rules 147, 144, 143) are cases of this kind and call for explanation by the cataloguer.

e.g. Title-page wanting. Caption title used.
e.g. Added title-page in Russian.
e.g. Afterwards issued under title *My son, my son*.

Peculiar features of imprint or collation will also require notes. The date may vary in different volumes; copies may be limited in number; the book may be a photostat copy. There may be irregular paging; plates loose in pockets; maps on the end papers; pages or illustrations missing.

e.g. Vol. 1. 1889; v.2, 1891; v.3, 1901.
e.g. Only 250 copies printed.
e.g. P. 105–120 missing.

The presence of bibliographies should be noted, also changes in a new edition.

e.g. Bibliog. p. 251–253.
e.g. List of translations used: p. ix–x.
e.g. Chapters 1–7 and 23 entirely rewritten.

Literary annotation is often described as a "descriptive extension of the title-page." It may give an author's qualifications for writing the book, *e.g.* his degrees, or the fact that he lived for twenty years in the country he describes. It may explain an enigmatic or misleading title, indicate whether the book has a popular or limited appeal, or mention an earlier work to which it is a sequel. Two books published close together were called *The golden fleece*, but one dealt with the Argonauts and the other with sheep farming. An astronomy book may require a knowledge of mathematics and physics before the reader can understand it. Lockhart's *Retreat from glory* is a continuation of the author's life which was begun in *Memoirs of a British agent*.

Below are examples of both kinds of notes. They have been taken at random from an issue of *The reader's index and guide*, produced by the Croydon Public Libraries. Only author, brief title, and the note are quoted in each case.

(1) BOAS, F. S. (*Ed.*). Songs and Lyrics from the English Playbooks.
   From the Middle Ages to the end of the Nineteenth Century.

(2) BRITTEN, Benjamin. Peter Grimes: an opera in three acts . . .
   Vocal score with piano accompaniment.

(3) BRUNNER, Emil. Justice and the Social Order . . .
   Prof. B. is a Swiss theologian. An "attempt to establish a doctrine of justice on Protestant principles" setting forth "what is required as just by Christian faith" in the fields of sociology and politics.

(4) DU MAURIER, Daphne. The years between: a play . . .
   Characters: 5 men, 4 women, a ten-year-old boy. Scene: the library of an old country manor house. Period: 1942–5.

(5) EDLER, J. M. History of Photography.
   Tr. from the German "Geschichte der Photographie," ed.4, 1932.

(6) JOAD, C. E. M. Opinions.
   Essays on religion, death, the birth rate, education, broadcasting, culture, politics, war, and the post-war world.

96   FUNDAMENTALS OF PRACTICAL CATALOGUING

(7) LATTIMORE, Owen. Solution in Asia.
>Far Eastern problems discussed from the American point of view.

(8) MATTIELLO, J. J. (*Ed*.). Protective and Decorative Coatings: paints, varnishes, ... V.1-2.
>V.1, Raw Materials for Varnishes and Vehicles. V.2, Raw Materials: pigments, metallic powders and metallic soaps. To be publ. in 5 v. Bibliog. refs.

(9) OMMANNEY, F. D. Flat-Top: the story of an escort carrier.
>Author was her Meteorological officer during a convoy voyage to Russia.

Notes (1), (2), (5), and the mixture of contents and bibliographical facts in (8), give information that is important for the student. The note to (4) is a useful guide to would-be amateur producers or secretaries of play-reading societies. Facts about the authors appear in (3) and (9), while subject-matter is explained in (3), (6), and (7). No. (7) also shows from what viewpoint the work has been written.

The following are taken from the *Music, Drama and the Cinema* section of a Derbyshire County Library Book List.

>Conductor's gallery. Donald Brook. 1945.
>>Biographical sketches of contemporary orchestral conductors.
>
>From art to theatre. G. R. Kernodle. 1944.
>>Concludes that the forms and conventions of the Renaissance Theatre are derived from the traditions of the visual arts.
>
>How to become a comedian. Lupino Lane. 1945.
>>Professional advice on technique for amateur comedians.
>
>A "Macbeth" production. John Masefield. 1945.
>>An answer to a party of young men, released from the wars, who seek for Masefield's advice on the production of "Macbeth" to village audiences.
>
>Philharmonic decade. Thomas Russell. 1944.
>>A history of the London Philharmonic Orchestra.

The type of note used here is only concerned with clarification of the book's subject. It suits the reader who has to choose

CONTENTS. NOTES. ANALYTICS 97

books from a list, because he is some distance from a library branch or the headquarters. The chief aim is obviously to stimulate reading interests and appeal to the "leisured" rather than "student" type of borrower.

Quite different in character are the notes in a printed catalogue of Bibles issued by the Bristol Libraries. These rare specimens were on exhibition at the Central Library.

e.g. Lindisfarne Gospels; with introduction by E. G. Miller . . .
    Latin vulgate version, written about A.D. 690–700 in honour of St. Cuthbert (died 687), by Eadfrith, his successor in the See of Lindisfarne.

e.g. Biblia Sacra, Hebraice, Graece & Latine . . .
    The Heidelberg Triglot. The New Testament was not published in this edition.
    Contains the autograph and MS. note of Archbishop Mathew in both volumes.

e.g. Biblia Sacra Vulgatae Editionis Sixti V. Pont. Max. . . .
    The Clementine Bible. The Bible of Clement VIII which remains to the present day the standard Bible of the Roman Church.
    The title-page is engraved.

Notes will vary according to the type of material in a library, the type of reader, and the form of catalogue. The student requires an annotation that will enable him to assess the value of a particular book in his line of study, while the leisured reader requires something to stimulate his interest. Notes in a card or sheaf catalogue will be briefer than those in a typed or printed book list.

Non-book material, like maps, gramophone records, microfilms, will require special notes supplementary to the catalogue entry, or instead of the usual collation items. In the case of a single map, collation is limited to size, which must be given across the open map as well as down. The scale, the presence of insets, and whether plain or coloured, are points upon which notes should be made.

e.g. Scale: ½ in. to 1 m. Inset maps on same scale for (1) North Yell and Unst (2) Foula (3) Fair Isle. Coloured Reduced by permission from the Ordnance Survey with local revision to date of publication.

Old, rare maps, like incunabula and other rare books, have notes describing any decorations and embellishments.

e.g. At top centre left: Cartouche, containing title, with decoration of strap work and fruit. Upper right corner: Cartouche, containing list of the countries, cities, bishoprics, etc. At side are the arms of Great Britain, supported by the lion and unicorn. Lower right corner: Cartouche, with author's name and imprint.

Certain faults should be avoided in annotation. The most glaring one is to give indefinite, and therefore useless, information. When describing a new edition, do not say vaguely, "considerably enlarged" or "new matter added," but "section on plastics enlarged by twenty pages" or "chapter on fungi rewritten." Contrast these two "popular" types of note for *China cycle, by R. P. Dobson.* (1) "Work in China before the war by a member of a tobacco firm, and an account of events and adventures during the war." (2) "A record of residence and travel in China from before the outbreak of the Sino-Japanese war until 1940." The second note explains which war and gives the exact date with which the book ends.

Redundant and valueless information should also be avoided. The fact that R. P. Dobson was "a member of a tobacco firm" does not help us to assess his qualifications for writing the book. He might have held a routine job that kept him confined to one small town; he might only have had the job for a few months. But there is some value in the author notes given in the Croydon examples. No. (3) is a book that deals with the subject of justice in accordance with the principles of Protestant Christianity. To be told that the author is a professor and a Swiss theologian makes one conclude that it will be, or should be, a learned contribution to this matter from the religious angle. If the note said, "Author is a professor of political science," we should assume the approach to be political rather than theological. A redundant note repeats information already given in the entry. It is surprising the number of these absurd examples which can be found in reading guides and library bulletins. For example, "Tells the amateur how to manage a greenhouse," when the title is *Simple greenhouse management*.

Finally, we come to the much-debated question of evaluation. Should the cataloguer give praise to the "best books" (or what he considers "best books") and condemn others as unreliable or commonplace? May he use adjectives like "comprehensive," "fascinating," "well-written," or "slight," "dull," "slipshod style," etc.? The type of short book list that is only intended for circulation during its topical interest may include evaluations, but they are a great mistake in anything permanent. No libraries in this country have sufficient cataloguing staff to be constantly revising catalogue annotations, so that evaluations recorded in 1936 may be completely out of date when read in the card catalogue ten years later. No cataloguer can be an expert in all branches of knowledge, and even to be able to call on the services of other experts does not necessarily ensure unbiased opinions. Then it should be remembered that evaluative notes will only be used by a minority. Some borrowers will not take any interest in annotations, others dislike critical ones because they wish to form their own judgments. Extracts from reviews are also a waste of time, since there is no room on a catalogue card to give the different opinions of several critics. Neither is there space for a sufficiently long excerpt from even one review.

To sum up, notes should be clear, concise, definite, and be restricted to information that is essential and only explanatory. Any attempt to evaluate the book's merits or demerits is outside the province of the catalogue.

3. ANALYTICS

An analytical entry is the "entry of some part of a book or of some article contained in a collection (volume of essays, serial, etc.), including a reference to the publication which contains the article or work entered." In this chapter, only author and title analytics are considered. Subject ones are dealt with in Chapter VII.

Eight modern plays, selected and edited by John Hampden. These plays are by different writers, so a separate analytical entry under author and title may be made for each (*see* Examples 50 and 51, page 101).

The analytical entry must always contain a reference to the work in which the analytic appears. This reference is put in parentheses, starts on the following line, and contains *In* (in italics), heading, brief title, and date of the main work, and the pages occupied by the analytic.

When unit cards are used, analytical entries are often made by using the standard entry card, adding an extra heading and underlining the particular part. Although a time-saving device it is only to be recommended for purely author catalogues. The set-out is unsuitable for title (and subject) entries as it gives the wrong sub-heading. Instead of DISCOVERY with the main heading underneath OULD, Hermon, this main heading would be HAMPDEN, John, *ed*. This is very misleading for anyone looking up the play by title, as he or she may conclude Hampden is the author.

Two or more works published separately and then bound together should not have analytical treatment. Each is an independent work, with its own title-page and pagination. The joining of the two in one volume is only a binding convenience. Therefore, each is catalogued as in ordinary cases, but an appropriate note must be added beneath the entry. "With this is bound . . ." and author and title of the second work given; three dots may indicate the presence of third and subsequent ones. For a second or subsequent work, add "Bound with" and give author and title of the first in the volume.

EXAMPLES

50

	OULD	, Hermon.
		The discovery, by Hermon Ould.
	(In	HAMPDEN, John, ed. Eight
	mode	rn plays. [n.d.] p.81-96)

Author analytical entry.

51

		DISCOVERY.
	OULD	, Hermon.
		The discovery, by Hermon Ould.
	(In	HAMPDEN, John, ed. Eight
	mode	rn plays. [n.d.] p.81-96)

Title analytical entry.

CHAPTER VII

SUBJECT CATALOGUING

1. SUBJECT ENTRY

THE A.A. code covers only author and title entries, so a definition for subject entry must be sought in the earlier *Rules for a dictionary catalog, by C. A. Cutter. Third edition. 1891.* This gives "registry under the name selected by the cataloger to indicate the subject"—a definition that is incomplete, since symbols of a book classification scheme can be used instead of subject names. For example, a book on the emotions can have subject entry under the word EMOTIONS; or, under 157 (Dewey Decimal classification), BF575 (Library of Congress classification), etc.

When symbols (*i.e.* class marks) are used for headings and then arranged in a catalogue, the order of the entries follows that of the classification scheme, *e.g.* 157 follows 156 and precedes 158. In Dewey, the subdivisions 150 to 159 are allotted to psychology and its various branches; the divisions 100 to 199 cover the bigger group, philosophy, of which psychology is a part. Instead of using a combination of numerals, like 157, this could be expressed in subject names. A separating dash indicates sub-heading and sub-sub-heading, *e.g.* PHILOSOPHY—Psychology—Emotions. Entry under this long heading, or under the class mark 157, is class entry, *i.e.* "registering a book under the name of its class." We get similar groupings in author and title, as well as subject entry, *e.g.* GREAT BRITAIN. *Board of education. Committee of the secondary schools examination council. e.g.* BIBLE. *New Testament. Epistle to the Galatians.*

Specific entry is the opposite of class entry; *e.g.* EPISTLE TO THE GALATIANS, or, GALATIANS, Epistle to the; *e.g.* DUNDAS,

Lawrence John Lumley, 2nd *marquess of Zetland*; *e.g.* MEMORY. The first two are as specific as possible in author or title entry. If used as subject headings, their extension might be lessened further, *e.g.* GALATIANS, Epistle to the, Criticism of; and DUNDAS, Lawrence John Lumley, 2nd *marquess of Zetland*, Life of. A book on the memory might only deal with methods for aiding the memory, *i.e.* mnemonics. In that case, specific subject entry would be under the word MNEMONICS. Entry under MEMORY—Mnemonics, or under the Dewey class mark 154.1, would be class subject entry.

These distinctions are very important in subject work because subject catalogues should follow one or the other principle. Two varieties, (*a*) *Classified* and (*b*) *Alphabetical-Classed* only contain class entries. Books on algebra are entered under 512 (if the Dewey scheme is used) in (*a*), and under SCIENCE—Mathematics—Algebra in (*b*). Again, (*a*) uses 733.5 and (*b*) the long heading, FINE ARTS—Sculpture—Classical—Roman, for works on Roman sculpture. On the other hand, the rule of "specific entry whenever possible" dominates the *Alphabetical-Subject* catalogue. There, entry would be under the name ALGEBRA or ROMAN SCULPTURE. Sometimes a library has an independent Alphabetical-Subject catalogue, but more often it amalgamates this with the Author-Title catalogue, and the combination is called a *Dictionary* catalogue. In this case, the subject entries become "added," the main entry still being the author one.

2. ASSIGNING HEADINGS

The student should first realize that more subject entries may be required for a book than is usual in author and title cataloguing. Much depends on the character and stock of a library. A special library may require more subject entries for books than a general library, since it wishes to draw attention to all material concerned with its speciality and will therefore make analytics on a much larger scale. The cataloguer has to use his or her judgment in this respect. In a general library, it would be absurd to multiply entries so that every subject aspect of every work was covered. A book like Margaret Mann's *Introduction to cataloging and the classification of books* requires entry under each of the two subjects; but whether analytics should be made for the varying sections of the Royal geographical society's *Hints to travellers*; or four added entries for *My wanderings in Holland, Belgium, France and Spain*, is a matter of individual library policy.

When words are used for subject headings, these need not be limited to the ones expressed in the book's title. This peculiar convention was followed in the early days of the Dictionary catalogue and is still practised in German libraries. As far as British and American cataloguers are concerned, its death-blow was dealt by Cutter in Rule 172. "Enter books under the word which best expresses their subject, whether it occurs in the title or not." He adds a long note about this "delusion," pointing out that such a practice means there can be no entry for books whose titles do not mention the subject. "A man who is looking up the history of the Christian church does not care in the least whether the books on it were called by their authors church histories or ecclesiastical histories; and the cataloger also should not care if he can avoid it. The title rules the title-catalog; let it confine itself to that province."

The cataloguer should always be wary of assessing subject from the title. True, titles should be—and indeed often are—exact statements of subject, but one never can rely on them. A book by J. N. D. La Touche, entitled *The young engineer* deals with railway construction in India and the Colonies, not with engineering in general. The subject of *Green armour*, by Osmar White, is not armour but World war II in New

Guinea and the Solomons. Titles like *Give back my rivers and hills, In search of two characters, Left hand, right hand!* give no idea of subject. Sometimes there is an explanatory sub-title which helps. In any case, it is better for the cataloguer to play for safety and not rely on the title-page alone. To assess subject, a book's chapter headings and table of contents should be examined thoroughly. The preface is also useful, as it often states the author's aims and viewpoint. Only when the subject is very elusive is it necessary to read the text or to consult reviews.

There is no code of subject cataloguing later than Cutter's *Rules for a dictionary catalog*. These have not been revised since the third edition was published in 1891. Consequently, they are too old-fashioned to be followed without reference to modern practice, especially that of the Library of Congress. No rules exist for either type of Classed catalogue, but the chief guide for the Classified will naturally be the classification scheme that is used.

3. THE CLASSIFIED CATALOGUE

Book classification has one strong advantage over an alphabetical arrangement of specific subjects. In the former, like subjects come—or should come—together, and a broad subject, like philosophy, is followed by all its branches. Instead of entries for books on algebra and arithmetic being in a catalogue drawer labelled A, those on geometry in G, and general mathematical works in M, we have a division MATHEMATICS with special sectional subjects, like arithmetic, as subdivisions. The value of a Classified catalogue will naturally depend on the scheme itself. A bad scheme will produce a very poor catalogue. It is impossible to enter into the merits and demerits of individual book classifications here.

The widely used Dewey scheme has been used in this chapter to illustrate types of entry.

The only possible headings for entry in the Classified catalogue are class marks taken from the scheme. Sub-headings may be names of authors and title words, but they will only form an author or title arrangement under the subject. As even a specific subject like elephants may have entries for several books, some sub-arrangement is needed for a number of cards which all bear the class mark heading 599.61. Class marks may represent form as well as subject, but form entry is discussed in section 6 of this chapter. What the student must realize is that the main entry is subject (and occasionally form), not author or title. Added entries in the Classified catalogue will only be needed when a book deals with more than one subject. In that case, the class mark for the main entry heading is the one chosen for shelf classification of the book.

As subdivision under class mark is by author, the two can be given in the heading and be separated by a space of one centimetre (*see* Example 52, page 116). An added entry could be made for this book at 923.173 (*see* Example 53, page 116). To make it quite clear to readers that the book will not be found on the shelves at 923.173, a note could always be put below the added entry, *Shelved at* 326.973. This can also be given in an analytical entry (*see* Example 54, page 117).

Every classification scheme needs an alphabetical subject key. This is chiefly intended for the reader who wants to know where specific, as well as broad, subjects are located in the scheme. The index of Dewey's is very detailed and shows the different aspects of topics.

e.g. Stairbuilding archi.   729.39
              carpentry   694.8
              stereotomy   515.83

Stairs
	architectural design	729.391
	plans	729.5
	carved archi. dec.	729.5951
	moving mech. eng.	621.8676
	painted archi. dec.	729.4951
Stakes plant support		631.3452
	training	631.5461
Stalactites and stalagmites geology		551.92

Many libraries place a copy of this index beside the Dewey-classified catalogue. A reader who wants a book on a subject, say stalactites, consults the index and then can turn to the correct heading in the catalogue. All cards filed together with the class mark heading 551.92 will contain entries for works on stalactites.

It is far more satisfactory if the library makes its own index on cards or slips. The printed one will certainly contain many subjects for which the library has no material, and therefore no catalogue entries. For example, only a very large or highly specialized library is likely to have a book, or analytical entry, for the Sui dynasty in Chinese history, and it gives the reader a bad impression when he looks in vain for the heading 951.015 in the catalogue.

The index to the Dewey scheme has also suffered through its originator's enthusiasm for simplified spelling, *e.g.* bildings, morfology, valvs. In the 14th edition, most of these have been changed to conventional forms, but there are still such Americanisms as defense and hight, which irritate British borrowers accustomed to defence and height.

An individual index should be made on cards (or slips), one entry per card, and filed in a set of drawers close to the catalogue cabinet. No book titles or author's names are added, since this is simply an index of subjects, not a sort of hybrid alphabetical catalogue. The entry on each card is limited to the subject name and the class mark, *e.g.* ELEPHANTS 599.61.

References should be avoided unless a number of double entries will be saved through them. For example, there is no need to send a reader to another part of the subject index and again to the catalogue by making a *see* reference from SOLAN GEESE to GANNETS. Make two entries,

e.g. GANNETS   598.43
     SOLAN GEESE   598.43

If, however, the subject is a wider one and there will be a number of sub-headings, then a *see* reference may be made from the less-used term. For example, the Dewey index has five sub-headings under CELTIC and three under CELTS, and a reference from KELTIC, etc., *see* CELTIC, etc.

When a library does not have a separate Author-Title catalogue, then the Classified catalogue needs an Author-Title index. This again is merely a key to the catalogue. Each entry may consist only of an author's name and the class mark, or class marks, where entries for his works will be found in the catalogue (*see* Example 55, page 117).

This does not give the reader any idea of the heading for a particular book, so many Author-Title indexes also include the title as well (*see* Example 56, page 117).

4. THE ALPHABETICAL-CLASSED CATALOGUE

This type of catalogue is seldom used now. Long, cumbersome headings, *e.g.* PHILOSOPHY—Psychology—Memory—Mnemonics, are far more conveniently expressed by a class mark, like 154.1. An index of specific subjects referring to the long class headings or numerous *see* references have to be added, otherwise it is impossible for readers and librarians to find their way about the maze. Another of its disadvantages has been stated by Quinn in his *Library cataloguing*.

"The great difficulty both to compiler and user is to know

where the subjects leave off and the classes begin—in other words, whether a subject or a class entry is likely to be the one wanted. One of the best examples of this kind of catalogue is the late Mr. Fortescue's 'Subject Index to the British Museum Catalogue,' and he apparently experienced the difficulty of deciding, as for instance a book on the Elephant appears under Elephant, but a work upon the Elk must be looked for under 'Deer.' "

The *British museum subject index*, and that of the London library, are both catalogues, not as their names would imply mere indexes of subjects. Both go in for a large number of class headings, particularly the former. They are not pure examples of the Alphabetical-Classed, but stand as hybrids of that and the Alphabetical-Subject type.

5. THE ALPHABETICAL-SUBJECT AND DICTIONARY CATALOGUES

Subject entry for both these catalogues is distinguished by its specific nature. This fundamental rule was laid down by Cutter. "Enter a work under its subject-heading, not under the heading of a class which includes that subject." *Text book of conic sections* goes under CONIC SECTIONS, not under GEOMETRY; *Guide to the varieties of toadstools* under TOADSTOOLS, not FUNGI.

It will be noticed that a subject heading is not confined to one word. It may consist of two or more, *e.g.* CONIC SECTIONS, INORGANIC CHEMISTRY, TRIAL BY JURY, ILLUMINATION OF BOOKS AND MANUSCRIPTS. If desired, the phrase can be inverted, *e.g.* CHEMISTRY, Inorganic; BOOKS AND MANUSCRIPTS, Illumination of. A *see* reference must be made from the form not used if readers are likely to look up the subject in that form.

Although specific entry is the foundation of the Alphabetical-Subject and Dictionary catalogues, subdivision of a certain kind is permissible. Many works are written in a special "form." For example, an encyclopaedia has "outer form" because of its make-up definitions and concise explanations of subjects being arranged in alphabetical, or sometimes classified, order. "Inner form" means the way the subject is treated, *e.g.* from a theoretical or historical point of view Subject headings in the alphabetical-subject catalogue may also have geographical and chronological division. So, without breaking the fundamental rule of specific entry, headings like the following are permissible.

e.g. EDUCATION—Encyclopaedias
LIBRARY ECONOMY—Periodicals
MUSIC—History
BIRDS—Sweden
EUROPE—History—1453 to 1517

but not,

EDUCATION—Adult education
LIBRARY ECONOMY—Cataloguing
MUSIC—Instruments
BIRDS—Owls

These must be entered directly under the specific topic names, *e.g.* ADULT EDUCATION, CATALOGUING, MUSICAL INSTRUMENTS, OWLS. Where the name consists of more than one word, inversion can be made so as to bring the specific topic nearer its class group, but inversion must be distinguished from subdivision. Specific topics whose first word is the same as a form divided group, follow the broader subject, *e.g.*

Form subdivision.   MUSIC—Dictionaries
MUSIC—History
MUSIC—History—England
MUSIC—History—Germany
MUSIC—Periodicals
MUSIC—Study and teaching
Music—Theory

Compound subject names. Music, Dramatic
Music, Sacred
Music, Vocal
Musical Instruments

Use of the ethnic adjective is restricted to literatures, literary forms, and languages, since these are not necessarily connected with geographical boundaries and cannot be put under country. For example, American Literature, English Poetry, Dutch Language, but United States—History, England—History, Holland—Travel.

Plural names are preferred to singular when choosing terms, *e.g.* Horses, not Horse, The. Unless the library is a special scientific one, popular terms should be used rather than scientific ones, *e.g.* Liverworts, not Hepaticae. Words that are alike, but have different meanings should be distinguished, *e.g.* China (country) and China (pottery).

Cutter devotes twenty-eight rules to subject entry, but many of these need modifying and extending to be brought in accordance with modern practice. For example, he advocates double entry freely. To-day we rely on *see* references to direct readers from rejected to chosen headings. Where the subject has local treatment, entry under subject and under place bulks the catalogue unnecessarily. A library may have ten books on birds of England. This means twenty cards, if each one is entered under Birds—England and again under England—Birds. If only the first heading is used for entries and a *see* reference (*i.e.* "nothing here") made for the latter, this only means eleven additional cards instead of twenty.

The *see also* reference (*i.e.* "for further information . . .") is a very important feature of the Alphabetical-Subject and Dictionary catalogues. It serves two purposes. First, it directs the reader to material on other branches of a subject, usually the more specific subdivisions. In a classified catalogue, the branches Emotions, Memory, Sensation, etc., would be grouped under the main subject Psychology, not scattered according to the position in the alphabet of their first letters. Here they are linked together by a *see also* reference, and this guides the inquirer who cannot find all the material he needs under PSYCHOLOGY. Secondly, he is saved the trouble of looking up headings which will not appear in the catalogue. Other branches, like Imagination, are not included in the reference because the library contains no material specifically dealing with them.

"The systematic catalog," says Cutter, meaning both Alphabetical-Classed and Classified, "undertakes to exhibit a scientific arrangement of the books in a library in the belief that it will thus best aid those who would pursue any extensive or thorough study. The dictionary catalog sets out with another object and a different method, but having attained that object—facility of reference—is at liberty to try to secure some of the advantages of classification and system in its own way. Its subject-entries, individual, general, limited, extensive, thrown together without any logical arrangement, in most absurd proximity—ABSCESS followed by ABSENTEEISM and that by ABSOLUTION, CLUB-FOOT next to CLUBS, and COMMUNION to COMMUNISM, while BIBLIOGRAPHY and LITERARY HISTORY, CHRISTIANITY and THEOLOGY, are separated by half the length of the catalog—are a mass of utterly disconnected particles without any relation to one another, each useful in itself but only by itself. But by a well-devised net-work of cross-references the mob becomes an army, of which each part is capable of assisting many other parts. The effective force of the catalog is immensely increased."

In the Alphabetical-Subject catalogue, subject is the basis of the main entry. The set-out can be the same as in the Classified catalogue, except that the class mark will be a word, or words, expressing the book's specific subject. The Dictionary catalogue is, however, far more extensively used, so only entries for that will be set out below. In this catalogue, author, title and subject entries are amalgamated into a single file. The main entry is the author one, subject and title being "added." Subject headings are often put in red to distinguish them (*see* Examples 57 to 60, pages 118 and 119).

The *see also* card may contain the names of any other hobbies for which the library has separate catalogue entries (*see* Example 61, page 119).

Sears' *List of subject headings for small libraries* is a great help to the cataloguer when making subject headings. It has a valuable introduction, containing suggestions for the beginner on subject work and how to use the *List* effectively. *The Library of Congress subject headings* is another such list, but more elaborate than Sears'. Both contain some subject subdivision, which is not strictly in accordance with the specific entry rule. Students should endeavour to limit their subject subdivision strictly to form, place, dates, and a few set divisions that occur again and again, like *Lives, Criticism.* Otherwise, fall back on inverted phrases if you want to keep parts of a subject together, *e.g.* CHEMISTRY, Analytical, not CHEMISTRY—Analytical chemistry; EDUCATION, Secondary, not EDUCATION—Secondary education. The working copy of a tool like Sears' should be altered accordingly. Some of the headings which are very American may need to be adapted to British usage.

When using a subject heading list, the beginner must also remember that *see also* references are only to be copied as far as they affect the material in hand. After assigning the subject heading EPITAPHS to a book, one comes to make the *see also* reference. Sears gives instructions that *see also* references should be made from ARCHEOLOGY; BIOGRAPHY; CEMETERIES; DEAD, The; INSCRIPTIONS; TOMBS. Most of these are cognates and unless the catalogue is unusually elaborate, it is impossible to link up so many topics. Aim at providing a *see also* from the group subject of which this is a part, but make sure there is already at least one entry under that name. One can hardly put the message, "for further information, look elsewhere," when there is nothing there to start with. In this case make the one *see also* reference from HISTORY, which seems more appropriate.

6. FORM ENTRY

Form subdivision of a subject is of two kinds. "Outer" refers to the arrangement of a book's contents, *e.g.* an encyclopaedia of music. "Inner" concerns the standpoint, *e.g.* a history of music. There are many books, however, whose subjects are too numerous to be named but have outer form, *e.g.* general encyclopaedias. With others, the subject is not so important as the form in which it is presented. Milton's *Paradise lost* is read as an example of epic poetry, not as a contribution to the Genesis story of Adam and Eve in the Garden of Eden. It would be absurd to classify or catalogue such a work under subject. Thus, books of a very miscellaneous character and books where literary form is more important than subject—both of these are catalogued under form not subject, headings, *e.g.* QUOTATIONS; ENCYCLOPAEDIAS, English; POETRY, English; or ENGLISH POETRY.

7. TRACINGS

The importance of tracings (*i.e.* record of added entries and references) on the back of the main entry card was explained in Chapter II. If these are not recorded, a catalogue soon contains many "dead" and incorrect entries. It is very easy to overlook some of the secondary cards when a book is withdrawn from stock, or the catalogue entry altered.

In the Classified catalogue, it is sufficient to give the class number for added entries. Abbreviations such as A.E. can be used. Subject index entries need not be recorded, as it is

SUBJECT CATALOGUING 115

assumed that some material on the subject will be left. It is useful to note entries made in the Author-Title index, but great care should be taken not to withdraw a card from that index unless there are no more copies of the work in the library. Unlike a catalogue, a card in the index may represent several copies of varying editions and dates.

The author card is the main entry in the Dictionary catalogue, so tracings must be made on the back of this. Full examples are given for the following:—

(1) History of Sweden / by / Carl Hallendorff, Professor in the University of Stockholm / and / Adolf Schück / . . . .
On back of title-page: Translated from the Swedish . . . by Mrs. Lajla Yapp . . . Preface, pages xvii–xxi, by Baron Erik Palmstierna . . .

(2) A / Treatise / on the / Coins of the Realm / . . . by / Charles 1st earl of Liverpool / . . .

The main entry for (1) is made under the heading, HALLENDORFF, Carl, *and* Schück, Adolf.

Back of card

Added entries.
    SCHÜCK, Adolf, *joint author.*
    SWEDEN—History
    YAPP, *Mrs.* Lajla, *tr.*
    PALMSTIERNA, Erik, *baron.* (analytic)
"*See also*" *references.*
    EUROPE

The main entry for (2) is put under the family name, which is JENKINSON.

Back of card

Added entries.
    COINAGE—England
"*See*" *references.*
    ENGLAND—Coinage
    LIVERPOOL, Charles Jenkinson, 1*st earl of*
"*See also*" *references.*
    MONEY

EXAMPLES

52

	326.	973 BROOKS, Noah.
	down by N G.P. port (Her	Abraham Lincoln and the fall of American slavery, by Noah Brooks... New York, G.P. Putnam's Sons, 1894. xv,471p. front.,plates, ports. 19½cm. (Heroes of the nations)

Classified catalogue—main entry.

53

	326.	923.173 973 BROOKS, Noah.
	down by N G.P. por (Her	Abraham Lincoln and the fall of American slavery, by Noah Brooks... New York, G.P. Putnam's Sons, 1894. xv,471p. front.,plates, ports. 19½cm. (Heroes of the nations)

Classified catalogue—added entry.

54

	550.2	BLANFORD, W T
		Section VII, Geology. (In ROYAL GEOGRAPHICAL SOCIETY. Hints to travellers. Sixth edition. 1889. p.336-349)
		Shelved at 910.2

Classified catalogue—analytical entry.

55

	STOKES, Alfred C	578
		589.47
		593.15

Classified catalogue—index entry.

56

	STOKES, Alfred C	
	Microscopy for beginners	578
	Key to the genera and species of the fresh-water algae and desmidieae	589.47
	Contribution toward a history of the fresh-water infusoria...	593.15

Classified catalogue—index entry.

57

	POSTAGE STAMPS
	CURRAN, Charles Robert.
	How to collect postage stamps, by Charles R. Curran. London, Hutchinson, 1934. xv, 296p. front., illus., plates. 19cm.

Dictionary catalogue—subject entry.

58

	STAMPS, Postage
	see
	POSTAGE STAMPS

Dictionary catalogue—*see* reference.

59

	PHILATELY
	see
	POSTAGE STAMPS

Dictionary catalogue—*see* reference.

60

	HOBBIES
	see also
POSTAGE STAMPS	

Dictionary catalogue—*see also* reference.

61

	HOBBIES
	see also
BOOK COLLECTING	
COINS	
POSTAGE STAMPS	

Dictionary catalogue—*see also* reference.

62

	JOHNSON, SAMUEL — Lives
MACAULAY, Thomas Babington, baron Macaulay.	
	Life of Johnson. (In JOHNSON, Samuel, Lives of the poets; ed. by Matthew Arnold. 1898. p.1-42)

Dictionary catalogue—analytical subject entry.

CHAPTER VIII

ARRANGEMENT AND FILING

1. NECESSITY FOR ARRANGEMENT RULES

BEFORE the advent of the printed book, catalogue arrangement was very haphazard. A medieval cataloguer dealt only with manuscripts which had no title-pages to guide him. Usually, he supplied a title by which the work could be listed. This might give indication of the author, or it might not. Many of the monastic library catalogues are divided into broad class groupings, but there is seldom any attempt at alphabetical or systematic order within the class.

When libraries were small and catalogues only mere inventory records, arrangement was not an important matter. To-day, a consistent plan is vital, and the larger the library the more detailed must be its rules for order of entries. The physical form of modern catalogues also makes it more difficult to locate items. It is possible to pick out a book title from a mass of unrelated items on a single book page, but no one can do this in a card catalogue where each entry is made on a separate card and filed vertically in a drawer with hundreds of others.

2. ALPHABETIZATION

Alphabetization affects the first arrangement in every type of catalogue, except the Classified. Entries in a Classified catalogue follow the classification scheme adopted, but there must also be alphabetical sub-arrangement under each class mark. For example, the headings for three different books on invalid cookery recipes will each have the same class mark (641.563 if the Dewey scheme is used), and then require further subdivision by author in alphabetical order of surname.

A clear set-out for headings, with key words blocked in capital letters, makes filing and consultation of the catalogue easier. By indenting two centimetres from the left edge of a card before beginning main entry headings, then a further two centimetres for added ones—the distinction between the two types of headings becomes obvious. It is also easier to sub-arrange the added entries.

e.g.   SING.
       ELDER, N
          Sing and play . . .
       SING.
       FARJEON, Eleanor.
          Sing for your supper . . .

The pitfalls in alphabetizing entries are far more numerous than the beginner would imagine. Hence the need for rules, and it must be emphasized that once rules have been adopted they must be strictly and consistently followed. First, the method of alphabetization must be decided. There are two of these, the *Word by word* (also called *Nothing before something*) and the *Letter by letter* (also called *All through*). The latter is easier, but the other is the one that is generally used in catalogues.

e.g.   *Word by word—*   *Letter by letter—*
       SOUTH Africa   SOUTH AFRICA
       SOUTH Australia   SOUTHAMPTON
       SOUTH Carolina   SOUTH AUSTRALIA
       SOUTH, Charles   SOUTH CAROLINA
       SOUTH Pole   SOUTH, CHARLES
       SOUTH Shields   SOUTHEY, ROBERT
       SOUTH, Walter   SOUTH POLE
       SOUTHAMPTON   SOUTHSEA
       SOUTHEY, Robert   SOUTH SHIELDS
       SOUTHSEA   SOUTH, WALTER
       SOUTHWARK   SOUTHWARK
       SOUTHWOLD, Mabel   SOUTHWOLD, MABEL

The *Word by word* method has certain inconveniences, especially in a Dictionary catalogue, with its mixture of subject and title entries. Words that sometimes appear as one and sometimes as two, may easily have entries scattered in two places, *e.g.* BOOK plates and BOOKPLATES, SUN dials and SUNDIALS. The same confusion occurs over prefixed surnames, *e.g.* DE LA Ware and DELAWARE, and through compound subject headings.

e.g.   *Word by word*—   *Letter by letter*—
      DE LA MARE, Walter   DEFOE, DANIEL
      DE LA WARE, Thomas   DE LA MARE, WALTER
      DE MORGAN, Charles   DELAWARE, ENID
      DE VERE, S.   DE LA WARE, THOMAS
      DEFOE, Daniel   DEL MAR, M.
      DEL MAR, M.   DE MORGAN, CHARLES
      DELAWARE, Enid   DEMOSTHENES
      DEMOSTHENES   DE VERE, S.

e.g.   HEAT, Conduction of   HEAT, CONDUCTION OF
      HEAT of formation   HEATHER
      HEAT, Radiation of   HEATING
      HEATHER   HEAT OF FORMATION
      HEATING   HEAT, RADIATION OF

When the *Word for word* method is used, there should be this modification, namely that the compound names of individuals, corporate bodies, and subjects should always be taken "all through." Hyphenated words are always regarded as one.

e.g.   DEFOE, Daniel   *and*   HEAT, Conduction of
      DE LA MARE, Walter   HEAT, Radiation of
      DELAWARE, Enid   HEATHER
      DE LA WARE, Thomas   HEATING
      DEL MAR, M.   HEAT OF FORMATION
      DE MORGAN, Charles   HEAT OF SUN

Apostrophes, as well as hyphens, are ignored in alphabetical arrangement. For example, *The boys' and girls' book*, *The boy's King Arthur*, and *Boys of '76*, all have title entry under the heading BOYS. Abbreviations, such as Mc., St., etc., are spelled out in full, *e.g.* MACLAREN, M'LAREN, and MCLAREN are all filed as MACLAREN. The umlaut in German words is also arranged as ae, oe, ue. Figures in a book title are treated as words, *e.g.* 1066 *and all that* is read as *Ten sixty-six and all that*, and filed under the heading TEN.

If the *Word for word* method is adopted, then only the word, or combination of words, to be used for the first alphabetical grouping should be in block capitals, *e.g.* LANE, Thomas, *not* LANE, THOMAS. This means that most personal authors will be arranged first by surnames, and only sub-arranged by forenames. Intervening titles, like Lady or Sir, are italicized (or underlined in a written or typed catalogue) and then ignored. Thus, LANE, *Sir* Henry comes between LANE, Harold and LANE, Hubert, *not* after LANE, Samuel. Initials come before full names, *e.g.* LANE, W T before LANE, Walter E. When an author has no surname, the first forename usually becomes the entry word and this only is blocked, *e.g.* ALBERT Victor Christian Edward, *prince, duke of Clarence and Avondale*.

Compound names for corporate bodies are blocked and filed through, *e.g.* LONDON MATHEMATICAL SOCIETY, but where the body is entered under place, only block the place name, *e.g.* LONDON. National gallery; *e.g.* GREAT BRITAIN. *Board of education*. The full stop, or dash, breaks the arrangement, so that National gallery and Board of education are regarded as sub-headings. The italicizing of government departments is the practice of the A.A. code, so has been followed in this book. We then get the following order of entries:—

    LONDON. National gallery.
    LONDON. Science museum.
    LONDON. University.
    LONDON MATHEMATICAL SOCIETY.

124 FUNDAMENTALS OF PRACTICAL CATALOGUING

Main and added title entries have the first word (excepting an initial article) as heading. If several titles bear the same key word, further sub-arrangement is necessary. This will be carried right through the title, articles being included (after an initial one), numerals treated as words, and abbreviations as though in full. Below are seven titles sub-arranged under the same title heading VINDICATION. Cards would appear in the following order:—

> The vindication and advancement of our . . .
> A vindication of the answer to some late papers . . .
> A vindication of the answer to the popish address . . .
> A vindication of the authenticity of . . .
> A vindication of the bishop of Condom's . . .
> A vindication of the brief discourses . . .
> A vindication of the Celts . . .

Works by the same author will have similar alphabetical sub-arrangement under the author's name.

e.g. BALFOUR, John Hutton.
> Account of a botanical excursion . .
> Address to the Edinburgh medical graduates . . .
> Biographical sketch of George Wilson, M.D. . . .
> Biography of the late J. Coldstream . . .
> The botanist's companion . . .
> Botany and religion . . .
> Botany of the Bass . . .

3. NON-ALPHABETICAL GROUPINGS

A certain amount of systematic groupings is necessary, even in alphabetical catalogues. An Alphabetical-Subject, and the subject part of a Dictionary catalogue, both adopt a systematic order for their different kinds of headings, *e.g.* general, *see also* reference card, subdivision by form, subdivision by place, inverted headings. Under ART, this would give:—

ART
ART (*see also*)
ART—History
ART—Philosophy
ART—Societies
ART—Study and teaching
ART—France
ART—Italy
ART—Spain
ART, Ancient
ART, Religious

Should added and main entries be filed in one sequence? It is generally considered advisable to keep them separate, sub-arranging main entries by title and added entries by their main headings.

e.g. Main entry.
    LAWRENCE, Thomas Edward.
        Seven pillars of wisdom . . .
Added entries.
    LAWRENCE, Thomas Edward, *tr.*
    LE CORBEAU, Adrian.
        The forest giant . . .
    LAWRENCE, Thomas Edward, *joint author.*
    WOOLLEY, C L , *and* Lawrence, T.E.
        The wilderness of Zin . . .

Two authors with the same surname and christian name must be distinguished by dates of birth (and death, if deceased). They can then be sub-arranged chronologically. For example, CASSELL, Donald, 1899–1931 follows CASSELL, Donald, 1871–1939. An author who is entered under his forename precedes one with a surname. Thus, JAMES, *Saint*, comes before JAMES, Henry. Some scheme must be followed for authors of the same forename when this is the entry word. The usual order is saints, popes, sovereigns, princes, and commoners. Two kings, *e.g.* named James, would be further arranged alphabetically by the names of their countries. If both reigned over the same country, they would be put in numerical order, *e.g.* JAMES I, JAMES II, and so on.

For Dictionary catalogue headings that are alike, but different in kind, Cutter's Rule 300 prescribes their order in the catalogue as, "person, place, followed by subject (except person or place), form, and title." He says, "This order is easy to remember, because it follows the course of cataloguing; we put down first the author . . . Of course, the person considered as a subject cannot be separated from the person as author. As the place may be either author or subject or both, it may come between the two."

e.g.   *Person* (author or subject)   BACON, Francis, 1st *viscount St. Albans.*
        Person (author or subject)   BACON, Roger.
        Place (author or subject)   BACON, *Philippine islands.*
        Subject name inverted   BACON, Curing of.
        Title word   BACON.
        Subject name compound   BACON-SHAKESPEARE CONTROVERSY.
        Person (author or subject)   BACONSON, William.

Alphabetical sub-arrangement by book titles is sufficient for the majority of authors who produce several books. But when "complete," "selections," etc., are published, as well as single works, then a systematic arrangement must be introduced.

e.g.   Complete works.
        In original language
           By editor
              By date of publication
        In translation
           By language
              By translator
                 By date of publication

Part collections, Selections, Fragments.
  In original language
    By editor
      By date of publication
  In translation
    By language
      By translator
        By date of publication
Individual works
  Alphabetically by title
    By editor (or date of publication if no ed.)
Added author entries
  Alphabetically by author edited, translated, etc.
Added subject entries (*e.g.* criticism, biography)
  Alphabetically by author of each work

A special scheme for arranging the Bible and its parts is given under the A.A. Rule 119. This can be extended in a Dictionary catalogue to include subject entries, such as criticisms, commentaries, and concordances. The order is complete copies of the Bible, selections, the Old and then the New Testaments. Sub-arrangement under each of the two last named is first, complete collections, secondly individual canonical books, thirdly apocryphal books. Provision is also made for further sub-division by language.

4. SORTING AND FILING

Sorting is the process of arranging cards in exact order before they are filed in the catalogue. To do this the cataloguer puts them first into rough alphabetical (or classified) groups. If alphabetical, this will probably be by the initial letter of the heading. When this has been done, the A group will be subdivided into smaller groups, AA, AB, AC, etc. It depends on the number of cards whether a final sorting can now be made in exact order, or whether more groups must be formed.

Catalogue filing demands complete accuracy, since a card

that gets out of place will be lost. Worse still, its wrong position may lead another cataloguer astray and cause him to file others in front or behind it, thinking this is the proper place. Because the work is so important, frequent breaks are necessary for the filer. No one can maintain the required standard of accuracy and attention for more than an hour at a stretch. As regards speed, one business firm estimates that an assistant can file 225 pieces per hour, but this is far higher than can be expected from the intricate work of a library catalogue filer. Here speed should only be a second consideration.

The cards should be placed in their correct places in a drawer without the locking rod being removed. They will stick up above the others and can then be checked for accuracy of placing before the rod is drawn out. The cards can then be pushed down flush with the others and the rod replaced. A cataloguer should also check the labels and guides to make sure they do represent cards actually in each drawer, and as soon as a drawer becomes too full these must be removed to the next. This proper spacing is most important, since it is impossible to consult cards that are tightly packed together.

CHAPTER IX

SIMPLIFIED CATALOGUING

1. THE VARIED FUNCTIONS OF A CATALOGUE

AMERICAN librarians record instances of borrowers using the library catalogue to obtain miscellaneous facts that one normally finds in an encyclopaedia or a biographical dictionary. Such a function of the catalogue is outside the cataloguer's province. He is only concerned with the task of making it fulfil its essential purposes. First, does it show the library's complete stock from an author, a title, and a subject approach? That is, can it answer the questions, "Have you got a book by so-and-so?" "Have you a book with such-and-such a title?" "What books have you on such-and-such a subject?" Secondly, does it show the location of every book in the library? Thirdly, does it describe each book in enough detail for a reader to judge from the catalogue entry whether it will be of use to him or not?

This task is made easier or more difficult by such factors as size of library, method of administration, type of borrower, and even the type of book which predominates. Cutter recognized the influence of the last two when he wrote, "No code of cataloging could be adopted in all points by everyone, because the libraries for study and the libraries for reading have different objects, and those who combine the two do so in different proportions. Again, the preparation of a catalog must vary as it is . . . to be merely an index to the library, giving in the shortest possible compass clues by which the public can find books, or is to attempt to furnish more information on various points . . . Without pretending to exactness, we may divide . . . catalogs into short-title, medium-title, and full-title or bibliographic."

The student uses the catalogue to discover subject as well as author resources. He may also be particular about such points as edition and date of publication. The leisure reader is likely to regard the catalogue only as a finding list. "Has the library got this book? Where is it kept?" Some books are of permanent value, others of ephemeral interest. Are both types to be catalogued in the same way? Size and method of administration must also be borne in mind, since readers will depend far more on the catalogue in a closed library than in an open-access one. All large libraries have stack rooms that are "closed," so, as the stock increases, borrowers are obliged to do more "selecting" from the catalogue.

2. SIMPLIFIED CATALOGUING

The term *simplified* cataloguing is generally restricted to simplification of entry (heading and book description), whereas *selective* refers to making added and analytical entries in important cases only and even omitting main entries for "unimportant" works.

Selective cataloguing is not considered here since it is considered that the catalogue must provide at least a main entry for every book. If it does not, the catalogue cannot be a complete record of the library's stock, nor be a true guide to the location of every volume.

As regards the third function, book description sufficiently detailed for the reader to select from the catalogue, this may vary according to the character and size of the library. This is what Cutter means in his division of catalogues into short-title, medium-title, and full-title. Title, edition, imprint, collation, series, and annotations may be "simplified." The heading is not generally affected. But all libraries must fulfil the two functions of showing complete stock and location of every book.

3. THE HEADING (AUTHOR)

Some libraries favour the omission of christian names in the heading and only give initials, but it is doubtful whether such shortening is an effective economy. If the title-page only gives initials, at least spaces should be left for the full names to be inserted in the heading later, while if christian names are used on a title-page they should certainly be used in the catalogue entry. Time will only be wasted later in tracing names from the books themselves, as well as from reference works, when two authors are found to have the same surname and the same initial or initials. Except in very large catalogues, there are not a great number of writers with the same surnames and christian names, so that dates of birth and death need only be given when two of these have to be distinguished.

Generally speaking, simplification of the A.A. rules for entry is not recommended either. It may be found advisable to adopt the American alternatives for Rules 33, 40 and 41, as borrowers usually know the later forms better. As regards Rule 38, entry under the pseudonym is certainly better for popular modern fiction (*e.g.* John Rhode, not Cecil John Charles Street), and possibly for older authors who are better known by the assumed name (*e.g.* George Eliot, Pierre Loti, etc.).

4. TRANSCRIPTION OF TITLE

The title-page was first designed to attract would-be purchasers, not merely to show a book's subject-matter. Hence titles often contain unnecessary "puffs," *i.e.* adjectives which merely extend the title without contributing to a description of the book's scope. Another advertising device was to introduce phrases about the author, showing that he held a Master of Arts degree or had written other works.

A.A. Rule 136 says the title is "usually" to be given in full, but allows "mottoes and non-essential matter of any kind, as well as designation of series" to be missed out. Although Cutter is anxious that too much shortening should not take place, he emphasizes that by fullness he means information rather than actual words. "Many a title a yard long does not convey as much meaning as two well-chosen words."

A long title can be extremely confusing, even when seen on the printed title-page. Here, however, the printer can introduce various sizes of type in order to make the important parts stand out. In the second example given below, type sizes fluctuate between 6 point and 12 point, while some words have a distinct slope to the right. The whole effect is most irritating to the eye, but it does enable the reader to grasp the meaning sooner than he would if he saw it written or typed on a card. Also, card space is restricted and the cataloguer may be forced to continue a long title on a second, or even a third, card. Below are three cases of unduly long titles which would be difficult to read if they were given in full in a card catalogue. They are all taken from books published since 1850. Earlier books sometimes have even longer titles, particularly in the seventeenth century.

Examples:
(a) The / appraiser, auctioneer, broker, / house and estate agent, / and valuer's / pocket assistant, / for the valuation for purchase, / sale, or renewal, of leases, annuities and reversions, / and of property generally: / with / prices for inventories / and a guide to determine the / value of interior fittings, furniture, and other effects. / By John Wheeler, Valuer / Sixth Edition, / Revised, Rewritten, and Greatly Extended, by C. Norris, Surveyor, Valuer, etc.
(b) A winter cruise in summer seas / "How I found" health / Diary of a two months' voyage in the / Royal Mail Steam Packet Company's s.s. Clyde, / from Southampton, through the Brazils, to Buenos Aires and back / for / £100. / By / Charles C. Atchison. / Pro-

fusely illustrated with photographs, and sketches by Walter W. Buckeley.

(c) The / Bhilsa topes; / or, / Buddhist monuments of Central India: / comprising / a brief historical sketch / of the / rise, progress, and decline of Buddhism; / with an account of the / opening and examination of the various groups of topes / around Bhilsa. / By / Brev.-Major Alexander Cunningham, / Bengal Engineers / "Yon fabric huge, / Whose dust the solemn antiquarian turns, / And thence in broken sculptures, cast abroad / Like Sibyl's leaves, collect the builder's name, / Rejoiced." Dyer.—Ruins of Rome / Illustrated with thirty-three plates.

In this last example we have title proper, alternative title, two sub-titles, description of author's status, a quotation of five lines, and a statement about the illustrations.

In the 1941 Revised Code, Rule 226 gives instances where omissions may be made in transcription of title. These include name of author and series when given at the top of the title-page; statement of illustrations; titles of honour, etc., following the author's name; explanatory phrases preceding the main title when not part of it; and, finally, mottoes, quotations, and other non-essential matter. These directions do not actually help the cataloguer to abridge a long title, except for such obvious "cuts." Abridgment will vary according to full, medium, and short cataloguing, but there are certain principles which everyone should follow.

However short the catalogue, essential matter must not be omitted, or the reader may be confused or misled. As Cutter says, "The title must not be so much shortened that the book shall be confounded with any other book of the same author or any other edition of the same book, or that it shall fail to be recognized by those who know it . . . or that it shall convey a false or insufficient idea of the nature of the work . . ." Certainly, the cataloguer should always retain anything which (*a*) explains the subject, provided this has not already been explained; (*b*) shows method of treatment, or for what type of reader the work is intended.

e.g. (*a*) The lady of the hare: a study in the healing power of dreams.
Agricultural analysis: a handbook of methods, excluding those for soils.
View of the state of Europe during the middle ages.
(*b*) Capital punishment, from the Christian standpoint.
Preparatory English course for the foreign student.

Cutter urges retention of an alternative title, in case some readers only know the book by this. Such an instance must be very rare. Alternative titles are not popular with modern authors, but they had a great vogue until recent years. Often they are useless in contributing any description of the book's nature, but sometimes they combine the function of a sub-title and are explanatory, *e.g. St. Paul in Britain; or, The origin of British as opposed to papal christianity.* In a short or a medium catalogue they may be missed out.

Short and medium catalogues may also omit the author's name from the title, provided this form does not differ materially from that in the heading. It does not matter if the heading has Pierre Joseph van Beneden and the title P. J. van Beneden. But when the title-page gives "by Edward White, archbishop" and the heading is "BENSON, Edward White, *abp. of Canterbury*," then "by Edward White, archbishop" must be included in the title transcription. Another case where repetition is needed is to make the title details clear. Take as an example, *The higher life in art, with a chapter on hobgoblins by the great masters. By Wyke Bayliss.* If "By Wyke Bayliss" is omitted, someone may think the phrase "by the great masters" refers to authorship of the book.

Those parts of the title which give redundant information may certainly be missed out in medium and short catalogues.

Full might also consider such shortening if it saves carrying on to a second card. For example, a sub-title "being a treatise on the nature of energy" is not much use when appended to a title, "Energy and its laws." Another example is as follows: *How to grow cucumbers: a practical account of the cultivation of a profitable crop.*

Much depends on the nature of the library, its readers, and its stock, but cataloguers need to guard against confusing a catalogue with a bibliography. Henry Wheatley distinguishes between the two and points out that as the catalogue is in the same building as the books, therefore its chief function is that of location. "It would be absurd to copy out long titles in catalogue . . . when the title itself in the book can be in our hands in a couple of minutes. Sufficient information only is required to help us to find the right book and the right edition." Anyone can copy title-pages, but it requires judgment and experience to "cut" properly.

5. EDITION, IMPRINT, COLLATION

The choice of editions, by Pearl G. Carlson, has this opening paragraph: "An edition is the total number of copies of a book printed from one setting of type. These copies may not all be printed at one time, for if the publisher finds that the number printed is not sufficient for the demand he may order more from the same set-up of type. These new copies, although minor typographical and editorial corrections may have been made, are known as new impressions or new issues and not new editions. Sometimes publishers use the word "edition" in a loose sense, meaning merely another printing from the same type set-up. This is certainly the case if a popular novel claims a tenth edition." Edition is only of use to the student when the text has been revised. Usually, the latest edition is required, but sometimes an older one may be asked for because it contains something that has been omitted from a later one. Except for fiction, the number of the edition (except the first) should always be given. This applies to all types of catalogues. Other terms, such as reprint, reissue, etc., can always be ignored.

As title-pages were first used to attract buyers, prominence was given to the name and address of the bookseller, who was also publisher and printer. Modern imprints consist of place of publication, name of publisher, often his address, and the date of publication. All catalogues must give date. Medium should give publisher, but only place of publication if outside London. Full gives all three items, but not the publisher's address.

The majority of cataloguers are sceptical about the value of collation in modern books, except number of volumes when there is more than one. Other items are pagination, details of illustrations, and height.

Few readers bother about pagination. Those who do are never interested in the distinction between preliminary and text pagings. The figures are supposed to give the reader an idea of the book's bulk and so enable him to pick a moderately thick volume instead of a thin pamphlet or a book too heavy to carry home in comfort. They can be very misleading. For example, the following combinations all come to the same total of pages, but they look different until one does an addition sum: (*a*) xiv,708p.; (*b*) xxxviii,684p.; (*c*) ii,720p. One is apt to assume from the catalogue that a book xii,566p. is twice as fat as one with the paging vi,283. But supposing the first volume to be printed on very thin paper and the second on thick bulky paper, the two will appear much the same until one opens the covers. Then is thickness a guarantee of worth? A well-written pamphlet may be a better contribution to a subject than some volume running to hundreds of pages.

Specification of illustrations often results in a mystifying string of abbreviations, which no borrower is prepared to disentangle, *e.g. front., illus., plates, ports., maps, diagrs.* Cataloguers in their zeal for accuracy worry whether to describe a plate as a photograph or not. What exactly are diagrams, facsimiles, etc.? A. D. Osborn, Chief of the Catalog Department of the Harvard libraries, gives the following amusing example.

"Thomas Thompson writes a book of short stories entitled *Lancashire lather*. The setting is a barber's shop, and the frontispiece depicts a barber. The cataloguer enters in the collation *front. (port.)*. There is no question but that it is the portrait of a real person attired as a barber; but it might be an actor dressed up to represent a barber; at any rate, it does not say 'Tom Smith' who could be verified as this particular Lancashire barber. Accordingly the reviser . . . changes the collation . . . to mere *front*."

Geographical students are supposed to use the collation to discover if a book has maps; historical students for portraits and facsimiles; and presumably mathematical students for diagrams. In all cases, it might be assumed that their books, if illustrated at all, would contain the type required. Certainly one never finds a geometry book without diagrams. J. A. Thornton, writing of a medical library, says that "most users of the catalogue know the medical subjects that positively demand illustration, and absence of plates is more worthy of note than the reverse."

Format is only given for rare books, but the A.A. code prescribes measurement of height for old and modern volumes. Width is only to be given when unusual. The majority of British libraries omit even height unless the book is oversize. Even then, it is surely sufficient to put a distinguishing letter (*e.g.* q. or f.) before the class or location mark to show that the volume is kept on the oversize shelves. Even American cataloguers seem doubtful about the value of the height in most cases, and can only justify it on such grounds as the following:—

"A literary editor engaged in reading a manuscript of a novel about the eighteenth century submitted for publication once telephoned me that he doubted the author's knowledge of the period, as at one point in the story the hero, interrupted while reading a classical author, was represented as hastily putting the book in his pocket. The editor's question was 'I thought all eighteenth-century editions of that author were either quartos or folios and even a hero can't cram a folio into his pocket.' When I offered to look up the question while he held the wire, he made the comment which lends point to this story. What he said was: 'Don't take any trouble, just step to your catalog and tell me if you have any edition of this work before 1800 which is less than 15cm in height.' As I reported one 14cm. tall the submitted manuscript passed on period accuracy."

Most cataloguers would prefer to have left their work—however urgent—to hunt for this information in a reference book, rather than make a habit of giving heights which could only be required in exceptional queries such as the above. Such a query is outside the real purpose and functions of the catalogue.

6. ITEMS TO BE INCLUDED IN THE THREE TYPES OF CATALOGUE

Simplified cataloguing should be confined to simplifying book description, not headings. A few rules may be modified in favour of "best-known" forms of name.

For the type of catalogue called Full, give the title as completely as is physically practical. That is, only omit items given in the Revised Code Rule 226, unless your title is abnormally long and will run to two or more cards. The rest of the entry should be according to the directions given in Chapters I and VI, but height may be omitted for octavos.

Medium should give the title shortened within the limits prescribed in Section 4 of this chapter, edition, place of publication other than London, publisher, date, illustrations (but not in detail), size if unusual, and series. Annotations may be added according to the library's requirements.

Short will be the same as Medium, but can also omit place of publication, publisher, illustrations, and series.

TERMS AND DEFINITIONS
SOME IMPORTANT DEFINITIONS

ACCESSION NUMBER.—The number given to a volume according to its entry in the Accessions Register. In this register, books are numbered progressively as they are added to library stock.

AUTHOR.—The individual or the corporate body responsible for the book's existence.

BIBLIOGRAPHY.—A list of books, or manuscripts, on a particular subject, or subjects.

CATALOGUE.—A list of books, or manuscripts, which belong to a particular collection or library. Such a list will be arranged according to a definite plan, as the following varieties of catalogues show:—

Alphabetical-classed catalogue.—Entry is made under the name of the book's subject, and is then grouped under the name of the class. The classes are arranged in alphabetical order.

Alphabetical-subject catalogue.—Entry is made under the name of the book's specific subject. These entries are then arranged in alphabetical order, *not* put under their respective classes.

Author.—Entry is made under the name of the author.

Classified.—Entry is made under the class mark which represents the book's subject in the classification scheme chosen. Arrangement follows the order of this scheme.

Dictionary.—Author, title, and specific alphabetical-subject entries are arranged in one alphabetical sequence.

Name.—Author, title, and name-subject entries are arranged in one alphabetical sequence. The subject entries are limited to personal and corporate names, *e.g.* for lives of individuals, histories of societies not written by officials, etc.

Title.—Entry under some word, or words, of the book's title.

TERMS AND DEFINITIONS

COLLATION.—The statement regarding the number of volumes, pages, illustrations, and size of a book.

EDITION.—All the copies of a publication that are issued at the same time and printed from the same set of type.

ENTRY.—The record of a book in a catalogue. Entries may be:—
1. Author, Form, Series, Subject, or Title.
2. Added, Analytical, or Main.

HEADING.—The word, or words, or class mark, which determines the place of an entry in the catalogue.

IMPRINT.—The statement regarding place and date of publication, and name of publisher (or printer).

LOCATION NUMBER.—This shows where a book is shelved. In a classified library it is usually the book's class mark, which may or may not be combined with an author or individual book number.

REFERENCE.—A direction from one heading to another. There are two kinds of references. The *see* reference means that the heading will not be used for catalogue entries. The *see also* means that the heading is used, but for further information the reader is directed to another heading.

UNIT CARD.—A catalogue card is made out for the main entry. Copies of this are used for added entries, the appropriate heading being added in each case.

INDEX

A.L.A. cataloguing rules (1941), 34, 50, 54-5, 61, 63, 79, 93
Abbreviations, 21-3, 33, 52, 63, 137
Accession numbers, 25, 140
Added entries
    author, 31-6, 38-40, 82-5
    classified, 106
    form, 114
    subject, 102-19
    title, 36-7, 41-3, 63-4, 70-1, 73
"All through," 121
Alphabetical-classed catalogues, 7, 103, 108-9, 140
Alphabetical-subject catalogues, 7, 103, 109-14, 140
Alphabetization
    "all through," 121
    "letter by letter," 121
    "nothing before something," 121-3
    rules, 120-4
    "word by word," 121-3
Analytical entries, 100-1, 119
Annotation
    bibliographical, 93-7
    contents, 91-2
    evaluative, 99
    faults, 98-9
    literary, 93-7
Anonymous works
    author discovered, 63, 65, 70
    author undiscovered, 64-5, 72
    "by the author of," 64-5, 73
    definitions, 60-3
    epics, 66-8, 74-5
    German practice, 86
    initials, 65
Arrangement, 120-7
Author catalogues, 7, 140

Authors, Corporate
    change of name, 80-2
    definitions and kinds, 76-80
    entries, 82-6, 89-90
    German practice, 86-8
Authors, Individual
    added, 31-6, 38-40, 82-5
    main, 13-30
Author-title catalogues, 8, 103, 108

Bible, 66
Bibliography, 7, 94, 135, 140
British Museum, *Subject index*, 109

Capitals, Use of, 16, 23, 51
Carlson, P. G., *The choice of editions*, 135
Catalogue cards
    filing, 128
    size, 12
    sorting, 127
Catalogues
    arrangement, 120-7
    functions, 129-30
    kinds, 7, 105-14, 140
    physical forms, 8
    simplified, 130-9
Change of name
    corporate, 80-2
    individual, 48-50, 56
Classical authors, 55
Classics, Anonymous, 66-8, 74-5
Classified catalogues, 8, 103, 105-8, 120, 140
Collation, 18-23, 25-7, 94, 97, 136-8, 141
Colophon, 8
Commentaries, 33
Compound names, 46-8
Contents, 91-2

INDEX

Corporate authors
    change of name, 80-2
    definition and kinds, 76-80
    entries, 82-6, 89-90
    German practice, 86-8
Cutter, C. A., *Rules for a dictionary catalog*, 7, 62, 88, 102, 104-5, 109, 111-2, 126, 130, 132-4

Date of publication, 8, 17, 24-5, 27, 136
Dictionary catalogues, 8, 103, 109-14, 124, 126, 140

Edition, 15, 24, 26, 29, 135, 141
Entry defined, 141
Epics and folk tales, 66-8, 74-5

Filing entries
    alphabetically, 120-4
    method, 128
    non-alphabetically, 124-7
    sorting, 127
    speed, 128
Forenames
    entry, 45
    initials, 13
    unused, 46
Form entries, 114
Format, 23, 137
Frontispiece, 8, 21, 27

Half-title page, 8, 24
Headings
    alphabetical-subject, 103-5, 113
    arrangement, 120-7
    author, 13-4, 32, 38
    classified, 106
    definition, 141
    form, 114
    title, 37, 41, 43

Identical names, 14
Illustrations, 15, 21-3, 27-9, 137
Illustrators, 33
Imprint, 17-8, 24-5, 27, 136, 141
Indexes to classified catalogues, 106-8

Individual author entries
    added, 31-6, 38-40, 82-5
    main, 13-30
Initials
    anonymous works, 65
    christian names, 13-4, 24, 28
Instruktionen für die alphabetischen Kataloge der preussischen Bibliotheken, 86-8

Joint authors, 34-5

"Letter by letter," 121
Library Association, Cataloguing rules (1908), 7, 12, 37, *see also, headings for individual rules*: Anonymous works, etc.
Library of Congress
    cataloguing rules, 21, 22
    Subject headings, 113
Location numbers, 25, 141
London Library, *Subject index*, 109

Maps, 22, 27, 35, 94, 97, 137
Married women, 48-50, 56

Name catalogues, 140
Nobility, 49-54, 57-9
Notes in catalogues, 92-9
"Nothing before something," 121-3
Numbers
    accession, 25, 140
    location, 25, 141

Oriental authors, 54-5

Pagination, 18-21, 24-5, 27, 94, 136
Periodicals, 68-9, 75
Plates, 22, 27, 94, 137
Pseudonyms, 54, 60-4, 71-3
Publication, Place of, 17-8, 27, 136
Publisher, 17-8, 27, 136
Punctuation, 16-7, 19, 26-30

Quinn, J. H., *Library cataloguing*, 108-9

Ranganathan, S. R., *Theory of library catalogue*, 83
References
    see, 44-59, 66, 80-2, 108-9, 111, 118, 141
    see also, 36, 41, 44, 80-2, 111, 113, 119, 141
    when to avoid, 108
Revisions, 34

Sears, M. E., *List of subject headings....*, 113
Serial publications, 69
Series, 15, 23-5, 29, 93
Simplified cataloguing, 130-9
Size of books, 19, 23, 137-8
Subject catalogues, 7, 103, 105-14
Subject cataloguing, 102-119
Surnames
    arrangement, 13
    changed, 48-9
    hyphenated, 46-8, 56-7
    prefixes, 46-8
    usage, 45

Title catalogues, 7, 100
Title entries
    added, 36-7, 41-3, 63-4, 70-1, 73
    main, 63-75, 86-8
Title page, 8, 94, 131, 136
Titles, Book
    abridging, 15-6, 24, 29, 131-4
    alternative, 17, 134
    definition, 14
    references from, 66
    sub-, 16, 134
Titles of rank, 49-55, 57-9, 61
Tracings, 32, 39, 43, 114-5
Translations, 33, 39, 67, 75

Unit cards, 31-2, 38, 42-3, 100, 141
Volumes, Number of, 20, 25, 30, 91, 136
" Word by word," 121-3

For Product Safety Concerns and Information please contact our EU
representative GPSR@taylorandfrancis.com
Taylor & Francis Verlag GmbH, Kaufingerstraße 24, 80331 München, Germany

www.ingramcontent.com/pod-product-compliance
Lightning Source LLC
Chambersburg PA
CBHW061844300426
44115CB00013B/2495